Praise for *Gratitude Practices for Teachers*

'As educators we face a raft of challenges. This guide to the practical application of deep gratitude doesn't promise to solve the systemic problems that teachers are increasingly facing throughout the world, but it does provide a glimmer of light, focusing on what we can influence immediately: ourselves and our perspectives.'

~ **Warren Brompton**, Primary school teacher, Canberra, Australia

'It is a book that helps us both appreciate and embrace every day, no matter what.'

~ **Dr Helen Street**, Founder and Chair, The Positive Schools Initiative, Australia

'Thoughtful, insightful and practical, *Gratitude Practices for Teachers*, is a must-read book for teacher educators, teacher students and all teachers working in schools. This is a book for any educator striving for understanding gratitude in everyday life challenges; it all starts with your inner attitude.'

~ **Solveig Cornér**, PhD, Teacher education programme, Faculty of Educational Sciences, University of Helsinki, Finland

'The exploration of gratitude practices for teachers is a truly transformative journey, skilfully delving into the immense power of expressing gratitude. The authors captivate us with their heartfelt narratives, resonating deeply and mirroring my own personal encounters.'

~ **Jessica Power**, Beginning teacher, New South Wales, Australia

'The timing of this publication could not be better. Bringing practical "next day in the classroom" ideas, it helps us all hone our gratitude practices for better outcomes for everyone in schools.'

~ **Bonnie Jeffrey**, Network Leader for School Principals, Department for Education, Children and Young People, Tasmania, Australia

'More than ever, our schools need gratitude roaming the hallways, cheering in the stands, and giving commencement speeches. This requires nurturing and supporting those on the front line: teachers. *Gratitude Practices for Teachers* does this via a practical, science-based approach.'

~ **Jeffrey Froh**, Professor of Psychology, Hofstra University, United States. Co-author of *Making Grateful Kids* and *Thrive*

'In this book, Kerry and her co-author Jo, show us how gratitude is a gentle yet strong thread for restoring our relationships and I recommend it to teachers at all levels of education.'

~ **Professor Ruth Shimmo**, Head of School, Tallinn University, Estonia

'I found myself frequently nodding along as I read, and mentally earmarking sections to use in my discussions with student teachers and early career teachers for whom I am responsible. It has also encouraged me (as a teacher of nearly 30 years' service!) to reflect and attempt to reset my work boundaries.'

~ **Victoria Allen**, Head of Oriental Languages, Secondary school, England

This book is very special. It will empower all who read it.'

~ **John Hendry**, OAM, Co-Founder of Positive Education and creator of Relationship based Education, Australia

'Relationships matter in a school landscape. Kerry and Jo's research and insights into the power of gratitude around physical, emotional and social wellbeing, and highlighting its importance in building and maintaining relationships, will be extremely helpful for teachers and school leaders.'

~ **Gail McHardy**, Chief Executive Officer, Parents Victoria Inc, Australia

'Howells and Lucas have amplified the perspectives of educators who bravely confront daily obstacles, providing practical and enduring gratitude techniques. This is an inspirational read that provides accessible and sustainable strategies that will empower you, even in the face of daunting daily challenges.'

~ **Michelle Summers**, Assistant Principal, Wellbeing Lead, Senior Secondary College, Tasmania, Australia

'This thought-provoking and practical book, based on research and evidence, offers an invaluable roadmap for teachers, leaders and support staff to transform their schools and classrooms into positive, engaging, and deeply meaningful learning environments through simple and practical activities and reflective tools.'

~ **Colette Bos**, Assistant Principal, Learning Community Leader, Roma Mitchell Secondary College, South Australia, Australia.

'If you are an early childhood teacher, this book is for you too! The challenges of teaching in an early childhood education and care environment are complex and as teachers we sometimes feel more and more stretched by the call on our expertise, particularly in this post pandemic world.'

~ **Rebecca Hand**, Director Early Childhood Education, Early Childhood Management Services, Victoria, Australia

Gratitude Practices for Teachers

Navigating the Everyday Challenges in Education

**DR KERRY HOWELLS
AND DR JO LUCAS**

© Kerry Howells and Jo Lucas

Published in 2023 by Amba Press, Melbourne, Australia
www.ambapress.com.au

Previously published in 2023 by Hawker Brownlow Education.
This edition replaces all previous editions.

All rights reserved. No part of this book may be reproduced or transmitted in any form or by any means, electronic or mechanical, including photocopying, recording or by any information storage and retrieval system, without prior permission in writing from the publisher.

Cover design: Tess McCabe

ISBN: 9781923116085 (pbk)
ISBN: 9781923116092 (ebk)

A catalogue record for this book is available from the National Library of Australia.

Disclaimer: The stories shared in this book are based on true accounts, however the names and in some cases the details have been changed to protect people's privacy. The material in this publication is in the nature of general comment only, and neither purports nor intends to be advice. Readers should not act on the basis of any matter in this publication without considering (and if appropriate taking) professional advice with due regard to their own particular circumstances. The authors and publisher expressly disclaim all and any liability to any person, whether a purchaser of this publication or not, in respect of anything and the consequences of anything done or omitted to be done by any such person in reliance, whether whole or partial, upon the whole or any part of the contents of this publication.

Dedication

For our daughters:
Amrita – K.H.
Adeline Cloud and Frankie Helen – J.L.

Table of contents

Introduction 1
Chapter 1: Time-poor 11
Chapter 2: Exhausted 23
Chapter 3: Perfectionism 37
Chapter 4: Angry students 51
Chapter 5: Toxic staff relationships 63
Chapter 6: Disgruntled and disengaged parents 77
Chapter 7: Belittled teachers 95
Chapter 8: Waste 109
Chapter 9: When the system fails us 123
Conclusion 137
References 141
Index 149
Acknowledgements 158
About the authors 159

Introduction

The challenges of our job as teachers are enormous. While we are invariably time-poor, we can also be facing any combination of angry or neglected students, difficult parents, toxic staff relationships, physical and emotional exhaustion, impossibly high standards, professional belittlement and more.

Complex answers are often put forward as solutions to these problems. As a result, teachers experience seemingly endless restructurings, syllabus renewals, red-tape policies, cumbersome behaviour management systems, data collection, reporting schedules and onerous professional development. These solutions often take us away from the main reason we are here: to teach and to teach to the best of our ability.

That is why we have written this book about gratitude. Gratitude is a simple, yet profound solution to many of the problems we are facing in education today. At their core, most of these problems call for a focus on relationships, rather than systems, because they are human problems that need human solutions.

While *Gratitude Practices for Teachers* does not aim to present a panacea that is going to fix all of these problems for teachers, it does offer an alternative and more elegant solution because it draws our attention to relationships. Over the past two decades, a burgeoning body of research has shown that gratitude is crucial to our emotional and social wellbeing and that its most important function is to build and maintain relationships (Algoe et al., 2008; Bartlett et al., 2012; Froh et al., 2010; Tsang, 2006).

Many years of researching and teaching gratitude in a variety of different contexts have further demonstrated that gratitude greatly enhances relationships between teachers and their students as well as colleagues and the wider community (Howells, 2012; 2014). Gratitude supports teachers to nurture robust and respectful relationships and to deal with the fractured or damaged relationships that inevitably arise in the profession.

Increasingly popular approaches to gratitude in education tend to focus on situations where gratitude is easy to access – when we feel well-rested and fulfilled by the rewards of our profession, for example. Or when we are actively remembering and sharing the golden moments of our profession with thanks and positivity. There is no doubt that the gratitude we feel during these times builds our resilience and increases our capacity to access joy and optimism.

However, almost nothing is available for teachers that shows them how they can practise gratitude in ways that are authentic, meaningful, relevant and accessible when they are feeling exhausted, stressed and overwhelmed. In this book, we will explore how gratitude supports our resilience because it does not shy away from adversity. Tackling challenges head-on, we offer a series of gratitude practices that teachers can engage with straightaway to support them with their everyday difficulties.

A practical, problem-based approach

The theoretical underpinnings of this book have been explored in depth in *Gratitude in Education: A Radical View* (Howells, 2012). This was the first book ever written that outlines a pedagogy of teacher gratitude. Using case studies from a variety of school contexts, this book presents a framework of gratitude that is highly contextualised and can shape our daily classroom practices.

While facilitating many professional book clubs and workshops that discuss *Gratitude in Education*, it has become clear how this framework helps educators understand how to apply important dimensions of gratitude in school contexts. However, the feedback received from educators has been that they need an additional text that can offer further gratitude practices for teachers facing everyday challenges. That is why we have taken a problem-based approach to this book.

Indeed, we have found that there is no better place to understand and experience the depths of gratitude than in situations of adversity. We offer a practical guide that can help teachers apply the theory of gratitude through relevant, context-specific gratitude practices they can employ even in the most challenging situations and within the scope of their busy, demanding and complex jobs. We offer a range of accessible strategies so gratitude can be a source of building resilience and teacher effectiveness, even when teachers feel their task is impossible.

Deep gratitude

Gratitude has many different meanings and is strongly influenced by our sociocultural background and life experiences. We acknowledge that many of you would not be starting from scratch and encourage you to start with your own understanding and practice of gratitude. In this book we offer a concept of gratitude that has been forged from years of considering the role that gratitude can play within the complexities and competing demands of education. We call this concept *deep gratitude*. We introduce four dimensions of deep gratitude which will be explored more thoroughly throughout the book: gratitude is an action; gratitude is about giving and receiving; gratitude is an ongoing practice; and gratitude is the opposite of resentment.

Gratitude is an action

Gratitude usually starts with an emotional response, a sense of appreciation, but then becomes more complete or deep when it is expressed as an action. In other words, we start with what we are grateful for, which has an inherent motivating force that propels us to express our gratitude to another. Grateful actions can play an important role in enhancing relationships and transforming school communities.

Importantly, we can see that deep gratitude and positive thinking are two very distinct constructs. Positive thinking is usually something that takes place on an individual level, whereas gratitude is highly relational. Deep gratitude is a powerful transformative force that connects us more fully and deeply to another. When we focus on what we receive from others, we awaken to an interconnectedness that makes us feel less isolated and less consumed by our own concerns. When we express this gratitude through action, it connects us at an even deeper level and grows our own gratitude.

Gratitude is about giving *and* receiving

Deep gratitude is also about the cycle of giving and receiving. These elements make it distinct from positive thinking, praise, positive acknowledgement or optimism. It is also these elements that make gratitude highly relevant to restoring a true dynamic to education. Students are no longer entrenched in the position of receivers of education but encouraged to think about what they can give. Teachers are not only focused on what they give but also on what they receive. Education is transformed from a commodity to a gift that we treasure and treat as a privilege (Howells, 2012; 2018).

Gratitude includes us in a particular kind of relationship with others. It is expressed with the intention of giving or returning thanks for what we have received in ways that are authentic to us and meaningful to the other person. There is also an important non-reciprocal dimension to this giving process: we do not need to give back directly to the person from whom we have received, nor do we expect it to be returned by those to whom we express gratitude.

As we will explore in the following chapters, for gratitude to have its truly transformative role in schools, we need to develop the art of becoming good at both giving and receiving gratitude.

Gratitude is an ongoing practice

When we are trying to express gratitude in challenging situations or difficult relationships, it is helpful to consider gratitude as a practice. Gratitude is not a quick-fix, one-off action and not something we need to get right the first time. As we explore in this book, we take up this practice with just one or two people and build our skills and confidence over time.

As discussed in Howells (2012), the notion of practice invites us to try something out, to train in it to become better skilled. When we decide to practise something, we are not considering ourselves experts. Otherwise, we would not need to practise. We become more proficient by regular, sustained commitment to our practise, however small it is. This reminds us that we need to be involved in conscious action rather than leaving it to chance and that this action cannot be dependent on our mood or the mood of others. When we consider gratitude as a practice, we also shift our perception away from the assumption that gratitude is about setting unrealistic demands on ourselves to be grateful to all people all of the time. Considered as a practice, gratitude removes that pressure and helps us to build resilience as we start accessing gratitude in areas where it is easy to feel grateful, before taking up one or two other gratitude practices in situations that are more challenging.

A crucial aspect of deep gratitude is that we take up these practices so that we can change ourselves, not because we aim to change others. As you will see when you take up your own gratitude practices, they help us to develop our character, integrity and resilience.

Gratitude is the opposite of resentment

We develop the notion of deep gratitude by drawing on the framework presented in *Untangling You: How Can I Be Grateful When I Feel So Resentful?*

(Howells, 2021). Gratitude becomes more accessible and sustainable when we view it in relation to its shadow side: resentment. We may want to be a more grateful person or to express gratitude to our colleagues and students but can feel like a failure when we cannot do this in difficult relationships because of our underlying resentment. It is often this underlying resentment that causes significant pain for many teachers. Deep gratitude is offered as a practice that acknowledges this challenge and shows how we can move away from resentment towards greater harmony in a step-by-step way.

Led by teachers' stories

In this book we share inspirational stories from teachers who have discovered the role of deep gratitude in navigating the challenging situations and dilemmas that many of us face on a daily basis in schools. In each chapter, we share the story of teachers working at the coalface to draw out general points that are relevant to educators. We also draw on international research which provides broader relevance for educators around the world. We have selected stories from different contexts, including teachers working across different disciplines; primary and secondary; inner city and remote settings; and early, mid and late career. The stories are based on true accounts, though all names and some contextual details have been changed to protect the individuals' privacy as well as the schools they work in.

Teacher challenges

In Chapter 1, we explore a pervasive and ever-growing problem for most teachers: being time-poor and the impact this has on our effectiveness as teachers as well as our health and wellbeing. Alongside Ben, we consider how deep gratitude might help us to establish a different perspective of time, review our never-ending to-do list and support and sustain us even when we are time-poor.

In Chapter 2, we introduce Lisa, who is end-of-term-teacher-tired. Looking around the staffroom, Lisa can tell it is not just her who feels this way. With Lisa, we discover how deep gratitude can help us navigate our exhaustion, foster our inner resilience and encourage us to recommit to the profession, even when we might feel that we cannot cope with the pressures of our job.

In Chapter 3, we consider John's story, a teacher suffocating under the weight of perfectionism. We learn the importance of expanding our gratitude by practising humility, embracing feedback and understanding the perfection of imperfection. Here we discover how deep gratitude can assist us to manage the unrealistic expectations we often set for ourselves and the extensive demands we feel required to meet.

In Chapter 4, we meet Abigail, who is faced with the seemingly impossible task of teaching Noah – an angry student who seems set on undermining her. Alongside Abigail, we examine how a state of preparedness and self-gratitude, as well as other deep gratitude strategies, can establish strong boundaries and support her to navigate this difficult time in her career.

In Chapter 5, we move on to staff relationships and learn more about the relationship between gratitude and resentment. We follow Hayley, who has become despondent as she struggles with backbiting and a competitive work environment. Through Hayley's experience, we learn about the interplay between gratitude and resentment and how deep gratitude can help us with toxic staff relationships.

In Chapter 6 we explore the impact of our relationships with challenging parents, including those who are overbearing and overly involved, as well as those who are absent or disengaged from their child's education. Alongside Josh, we learn how to use deep gratitude practices to grow our compassion and understanding. We explore how teachers can engage with parents, foster positive relationships and nurture communities of deep gratitude, even in the most hostile situations.

In Chapter 7, we continue the discussion around resentment in the context of teachers feeling belittled or inferior, using the example of ageism. We meet Margaret who is nearing retirement and feels undermined by new, energetic and tech-savvy teachers. We also meet Oliver who feels that his fresh and innovative approaches to teaching are being dismissed because of his youth and inexperience. Alongside Oliver and Margaret, we learn about the role of gratitude in helping us to build our self-esteem when we feel belittled and hold on to our integrity when it feels threatened.

In Chapter 8, we explore the environmental concerns that accompany working in education and how this may cause feelings of alienation for environmentally conscious educators. We follow Sophia, a teacher who feels ridiculed for her commitment to minimising the waste produced by her class and school community. We explore how deep gratitude can assist us and Sophia to care about and advocate for our environment even when we are surrounded by people who do not necessarily share our values.

In Chapter 9, we explore the dysfunctional aspects of the education system and how working in this environment can lead to feelings of oppression or hopelessness. Alongside Isaac, we consider how deep gratitude can help us to be more effective in agitating for change and speaking up about our grievances in respectful and empowering ways.

Cross-cultural differences

We are acutely aware that we are not explicitly addressing the cross-cultural elements of gratitude. Our exploration takes place within a Western context. We take stories from this context and consider the challenges and dilemmas experienced by teachers within it. Our suggested deep gratitude practices and their implementation also rely on this Western context.

We need to note that accessing, expressing and accepting gratitude can look and sound very different for people from diverse cultural and linguistic backgrounds. We recognise that, as teachers, we have a great deal to learn from culturally diverse ways of giving and receiving gratitude and that these need to be embraced if we are to be enriched by thinking about gratitude from others' perspectives.

Although a cross-cultural exploration is beyond the scope of this book, we invite you to keep this in the back of your mind when reading and actioning the theory and practices in your school. If you would like to read more about cross-cultural aspects of gratitude, this topic has been explored in *Untangling You: How Can I Be Grateful When I Feel So Resentful?*.

Institutional constraints

We also wish to acknowledge that we have not tried to address all the institutional constraints teachers deal with when trying to practise gratitude. We are well aware that sometimes it can feel like our efforts as teachers are meaningless because we work in a system that seems inherently broken. We can become despondent because we feel that the education system itself is getting in the way of us doing our job effectively: the endless paperwork; unrealistic demands on us as individuals; reduced funding and resourcing; complex bureaucracies, hierarchies and power dynamics; ever-changing curriculum initiatives, government policy, technology; and much more.

More broadly, systems that necessarily overlap with education such as child protection, health, justice, welfare and so on, may themselves be struggling to such an extent that they undermine the work we do and the ability for students and families to engage with education in a positive way regardless of our efforts as educators.

While acknowledging the real impact of these constraints, our approach is to offer a way forward where you can take greater agency. The deep gratitude practices we suggest aim to support you to take small steps forward by building a greater capacity to change the things you can change. In other words, our focus is on how we can use deep gratitude to empower ourselves to make the changes we *can* make, irrespective of institutional limitations and constraints.

How to read this book

Each chapter begins with an invitation for you to engage with some reflective questions about the everyday challenge we explore in that chapter. You may like to use a journal to record your initial thinking in response to these questions before you embark on the rest of the chapter.

We then explore what international research has to say about this challenge for teachers. Following this, we acknowledge the dilemmas teachers may face in contemplating the role of gratitude when they are struggling with the challenges of their work. We do this because one of the most significant barriers in thinking about gratitude is the scepticism that can arise if there is any suggestion that gratitude overlooks the very real constraints teachers are contending with in their work. We phrase this section as 'Gratitude. Seriously?'. We then reply to this concern with research that directly answers the question 'Why gratitude?' even in times of adversity.

Once we have established why deep gratitude is important, we offer a range of practices that are accessible to all teachers. As each gratitude practice is outlined, we offer inspiration and guidance from teachers who implement these practices in realistic and sustainable ways and gradually strengthen their capacity for navigating their everyday challenges through deep gratitude. We finish each chapter with a list which revisits the gratitude practices addressed in that chapter. This list is intended to support you to put gratitude into practice, prompting you to consider some accompanying questions and suggestions for how to develop deep gratitude in your own teaching context. You might like to return to your journal to record your thinking.

However, please note that we are not suggesting that you implement each and every gratitude practice offered in the chapter. As you will discover, just taking up one or two gratitude practices at a time is very powerful and achievable. Indeed, you might still be working on a gratitude practice from a previous chapter and choose to continue with this.

You may also choose to study this book with a colleague or a larger group. This has proven to be an invaluable process in building trust, collegiality and respect for difference as evidenced by working internationally with numerous book clubs on *Gratitude in Education: A Radical View* and *Untangling You: How Can I Be Grateful When I Feel So Resentful?*. It can give you added accountability and motivation as you support and encourage one another to practise gratitude when challenges arise. There is something powerfully enriching about deep gratitude that lends itself to reflection with others. However, the effects of your deep gratitude practices are not diminished if you choose to do these alone.

We understand that some chapters in this book, and the problems they explore, will speak more readily than others to the issues you are currently facing. However, we still encourage you to read the chapters sequentially. There are key concepts and associated practices that build on each other systematically throughout the book that will inform your growing understanding of deep gratitude. It's important to keep in mind that you are doing this work to grow and develop your own approach to teaching. This is not about changing someone else.

From the start, we also offer this caution to readers: please don't expect to get gratitude right in any finite or absolute way. We invite you to make a commitment to be kind to yourself as you experiment with and grow your gratitude practice over time. The last thing we want is for teachers to set themselves up for disappointment or a sense of failure by aiming to perfect or master gratitude. As we have already stated, we need to see deep gratitude as an ongoing practice.

We hope that the research, teachers' stories and wide array of strategies explored in the following chapters will support you to integrate gratitude more fully into your teaching and leadership, and that it will provide a valuable resource no matter what career stage you're in.

CHAPTER 1

Time-poor

I looked at my desk and shook my head. The piles of untouched paperwork were growing. I only had 45 minutes off class and according to my to-do list, I needed to plan a unit of work; contact parents; organise a class excursion; prepare a display of student work; mark spelling tests; nominate a student for an assembly award and email my principal about a performance review. On top of this, the resources I needed for my next lesson were not quite ready. I didn't know where to start. Feeling overwhelmed, I went to the staffroom to make a cup of tea.

Ben, Year 4 teacher

An invitation

What does your desk look like? How about your ever-growing to-do list? Do you feel pressure and stress when you add items to the list faster than you cross them off? Have you ever walked into a classroom filled with trepidation because you didn't have time to properly prepare? Do you regularly take a pile of unmarked books home only to bring them back to school untouched? Do you find yourself never really relaxing on the weekend or during the holidays because of work you need to get done before the next school day?

Being time-poor is perhaps the number one grievance experienced by teachers. We should not underestimate the impact of this grievance on our mental health and wellbeing, our job satisfaction and our effectiveness as teachers. In this chapter, deep gratitude is not heralded as a simple solution to this very real and serious problem. Instead, it is intended to offer hope as well as small, accessible, everyday steps forward.

We introduce Ben's story, in which we find a teacher who is feeling overwhelmed because he never has time to get on top of his to-do list, let alone do things well. We navigate Ben's journey through a series of deep gratitude practices that enable him to cope with the typical pressures of time-poor teachers.

How can we possibly fit it all in?

Ben is not alone. There is a great deal of international research demonstrating that being time-poor is an issue that affects many teachers. For example, in an Australian study by Monash University (Heffernan et al., 2019), 2444 teachers were asked to indicate their agreement with the statement 'I find my current workload manageable'. A large majority of respondents, indeed 75 per cent of them, either disagreed or strongly disagreed with this statement. Meanwhile, only 42 teachers, or 2 per cent of respondents, strongly agreed that their workload was manageable. A majority of teachers cited workload as a key reason for considering premature retirement, explaining that heavy workloads distracted from their core focus on teaching and learning, and had a negative impact on their physical and mental health and wellbeing.

Similarly, almost half of the teachers participating in the Organisation for Economic Co-operation and Development (OECD) Teaching and Learning International Survey (TALIS; Thomson & Hillman, 2019) reported that an increase in administrative work was a source of frustration and an unproductive use of time. For participating teachers, associated stress levels were linked to their intentions to leave the profession early (see also Boeskens & Nusche, 2021). Indeed, the administrative and data collection requirements of our job are rising exponentially, creating a 'tsunami of paperwork under which teachers are now drowning' (Fitzgerald et al., 2018, p. 613). This paperwork can kill our passion and enthusiasm, especially when it seems unconnected to teaching and learning. As an Australian study of 215 high school teachers found, non-teaching workload was a stronger predictor of burnout and job dissatisfaction than teaching-related workload (Lawrence et al., 2019).

Likewise, in the United Kingdom newly qualified teachers are leaving the profession as a result of the pressures of an increased emphasis on auditing and accountability (Burrow et al., 2020). This research also points out that policy reforms in the UK have rapidly intensified teachers' workload and the onerous task of completing paperwork. This study investigates the consequences of feeling time-poor, stripping teachers of the freedom to innovate as they deal with high levels of stress compared to the average workplace.

The time-poor teacher

Ben loved his job but every year the expectations and time pressures seemed to multiply. Over his seven years in the profession, the paperwork, report writing and record keeping had escalated. On top of this, he had to find time to keep up with frequent changes to the curriculum. In the past, Ben had kept a lot of his planning and assessment information in his head, but increased accountability measures meant it now needed to be organised, documented and communicated with other teachers and senior staff in a clear and coherent way.

The consequences of being time-poor became even more apparent when Ben made a significant error while organising an excursion to the local museum. It was the final excursion for the year and Ben put his hand up to organise it for his class and another Year 4 class. He immediately regretted his decision when he realised how much was involved in organising just this one event. The paperwork included a risk management plan; specific supports for students with disability; a printed map of the bus route to and from the museum; a class list of students for both classes; medical alerts; and permission slips on school letterhead, signed by the principal, scanned and then emailed home. Ben also needed to communicate with the museum; the school business manager to access funds; the front office staff to book the bus; the teacher aides who would need to attend the excursion; the whole staff to ask for a duty swap; the canteen manager; parents and carers to sign permission slips; and senior staff to plan for students who could not come on the excursion. All of this had to be prepared well in advance and Ben thought he had done well to get it done on time.

Two days before the excursion, Ben asked his class why permission slips had not been sent back. As he looked at the students' bewildered faces, Ben checked his emails and came to the shocking realisation that although he had prepared a draft email with the permission slips, he had forgotten to press send! The excursion would have to be cancelled. There simply wasn't enough time to get all the permission slips back. The ramifications were felt across the school. The students were disappointed because they had become accustomed to going on a field trip at least once a term and obviously felt let down. As well as being an important relationship-building experience, the excursion was also a significant component of their history unit and Ben realised that their learning outcomes would suffer.

Ben was disheartened by the wasted time and effort he had put into this excursion and the extra workload he had inadvertently created as a result of his mistake. He would need to prepare lessons for the unexpected day in class, create a new assessment task to replace the one he had organised around the excursion and communicate again with all staff involved to cancel the excursion. While he felt professionally humiliated, he also felt frustrated with the education system that put him and other teachers under so much pressure to cram too much into their working day, meaning that nothing could be done properly.

Gratitude. Seriously?

We recognise that for time-poor teachers like Ben, a suggestion to practise gratitude might seem like adding yet another thing to an unwieldy workload. In fact, many of our research participants have reported 'not enough time' as the major challenge to being able to practise gratitude (Howells, 2012). Though many teachers understand the benefits of practising gratitude, they feel the pressure of this as yet another demand. The stress of trying to fit in gratitude grows if it becomes one of the themes for the school year, part of the school mission statement or a compulsory component of an educational program or curriculum initiative. If gratitude practices become something we feel we must do, it's quite possible that we might start to approach the very idea of gratitude with resentment and bitterness.

Indeed, we have attended many compulsory staff meetings which have begun with participating teachers being asked to share a gratitude statement or write down three things they are grateful for. While these tasks can be valuable, when they are imposed on teachers in a superficial, platitudinous way, they can create cynicism and frustration. If gratitude is not well placed in the context of busy schedules and doesn't help with the immediate problem of being time-poor, recommended gratitude tasks are likely to be treated with disdain.

A further challenge for teachers is that they don't have enough time to 'do gratitude properly' (Howells, 2012). We might feel added pressure when we compare ourselves with others who seem to be more grateful than us. We might question how they find the time to practise gratitude when they have the same workload. Their gratitude can cause us to feel even more disheartened when we can't fit it in or do not seem to have enough of it.

Then there is the feeling that if we are grateful, we are covering up or excusing the systematic failures responsible for making us time-poor in the first place. Indeed, we might believe that overtly showing our gratitude could amount to failing our colleagues if they are struggling with unrealistic workloads.

Why gratitude?

When we are feeling time-poor, gratitude can remind us that getting the task done is not as important as the inner attitude we hold while we are doing the task. If we reduce gratitude to merely a 'thing', something that sits outside ourselves or something else to add to the to-do list, we overlook the transformative potential of deep gratitude. Deep gratitude exists in many dimensions of self. It is part of who we are – our feelings, our values, our disposition, our character, our habits (Howells, 2012; 2021). It is not an extra task but rather the spirit with which we take action in our daily life. It's a way of being and an inner attitude we bring to what we do (Howells, 2014).

As Parker J Palmer (2017) advocates 'we teach who we are' (p. 10). If who we are is flustered, stressed and pressured, this will have a greater influence on our students than the best-planned lesson. In this sense, gratitude is not a project with a beginning and an end but an ongoing practice of becoming more aware of the impact of our inner attitude on others. It is important to recognise that our sense of overwhelm can negatively impact our students, especially when we are time-poor. Even though we might be trying to get everything done to give our students the best teaching experience we can, what students need from us is our presence, not just the task we have prepared.

Sometimes it seems that the more we complain about what we have to do, the more difficult things become. If we bring an awareness of gratitude to what we are doing, we are more likely to consider our tasks as things we are able to do, rather than feel burdened by the things we have to do (Nelson, 2020). As we will explore in this chapter, gratitude can improve the quality of the time we have if we see it as something we have been given.

Research shows that gratitude brings many benefits to our daily lives. It leads us to feel more energised and to have embodied feelings of love, joy and awe (Hlava & Elfers, 2013), as well as an increased sense of positivity and appreciation (Allen, 2018; Wood et al., 2007). The joy our gratitude evokes can also reduce our stress and anxiety (Jiang, 2022; Tolcher et al., 2022). This joy opens us up to even more gratitude (Fredrickson, 2004). When we are open to what we receive through the practice of gratitude, there is a greater chance that one of the gifts we would be more conscious of is the time we have been given (Nelson, 2020).

Be grateful for time

Here we introduce our first gratitude practice in this chapter. When we feel time-poor, there is wisdom in taking an honest look at the time we have, our relationship with time and how we might be taking it for granted. In Ben's situation, while he was genuinely time-poor, he was also lacking presence for the tasks he was able to do. The shock he experienced in the fallout from the excursion mistake led him to think about where he could save time in his busy schedule. For example, he humbly acknowledged the time he wasted scrolling through social media. Ben realised he often did this even when he was trying to plan for teaching and learning and completing other administrative tasks. When he thought about it, he recognised a lack of presence not only in his work tasks but also in his everyday tasks such as eating and showering. His focus was on getting things done quickly and efficiently, meaning he didn't fully attend to what was going on inside of him, the people around him or his environment.

Like Ben, most of us have been guilty of wasting or misusing time. Not only do we find ourselves spending time on social media or binging on our favourite TV series, but also rearranging our room or our stationary cupboard for the third time in a week. Deep gratitude invites us to shift our perspective by approaching our actions with an inner attitude of giftedness, treating the time we have available as precious. When we do this, we become more fully present in our actions. If we want to express gratitude for the time we have, we can plan to use our time well and be conscious of using it intentionally.

On the other hand, when we take time for granted, we might find ourselves procrastinating. We put too many things on our to-do list without an honest assessment of the time it will take to do them. We can become so overwhelmed that we don't know where to start or feel so disheartened by the workload that we can no longer find the motivation to get anything done. We then avoid doing anything on the list or do other things to distract us, especially if they give us more pleasure.

When we become aware of our procrastination, we are invited to examine our relationship with time and reminded that we can't do more than our time actually allows. In being more grateful for time, we can be more realistic about the time we have and what we can actually achieve. This will support us to feel less stressed or overwhelmed and eventually help us to stop procrastinating because our to-do list becomes achievable in the time we are given.

When we are time-poor, we often treat time as an enemy or something we need to conquer and manage. Our language can be an insightful indicator that we have an unhealthy or combative relationship with time, obvious in phrases such as *stretched thin, too busy, under the pump, slammed* or *swamped*. Sometimes we want time to be our slave, expecting it to accommodate all the things we want to do in a limited period. In the end though, we are the ones who feel enslaved because we find we do not have enough time. By practising gratitude for time, we can work with time instead of against it and treat time like our friend rather than our foe.

Do one thing at a time

Being grateful for time itself would also mean that we could commit to doing just one thing at a time. Teachers are often heralded as being competent multitaskers. If we look carefully at the concept of multitasking, we can see that it is ultimately flawed. We know that for our students to feel our presence, for example, we need to bring our whole attention to them. However, this would be impossible if we are doing even one other thing at this time. Simply, there is no such thing as doing many things with our whole attention at one time.

Thinking of time and space as interrelated dimensions can help us grasp this point. We can see that time has the nature of being vertical. If we picture it as a mountain, we can only climb up one step at a time. In contrast, space is horizontal. Much of our dysfunctional relationship with time occurs because we treat time like space, where we do many things at one time.

If Ben had been more aware of the nature of time, he may have realised that he was doing too many things at one time in preparing for the excursion and may have avoided his mistake. As he was reflecting on his email communication about the excursion with families, he remembered that he was simultaneously talking to a student about their weekend and greeting his colleagues as they walked past.

In recognising that the pressures on teachers may well make them feel that they need to multitask, we should realise that if we do one thing at a time, it can actually save time because we do that one thing thoroughly.

When we bring greater awareness to the one thing we are doing, we are treating time preciously and therefore expressing our gratitude for time. We are more likely to pay attention in the moment and avoid letting our mind wander to things in the past or future. We can also bring our attention to what time gives us – capacity and quality to each moment that we are permitted to live. Gratitude also helps us to value our time and not take things for granted. We can treat time preciously and act intentionally as we complete each task on our to-do list.

There are some inspiring examples of practices that embody a commitment to doing one thing at a time in schools. For example, many schools in Japan have a daily ritual where teachers and students together clean the school or classroom at the beginning and end of each day (Luu, 2020). In many instances, they do this in silence with full attention to the task at hand and practise being thankful for all the materials available to them.

Keep it real

Ben's assistant principal had called him in to discuss an urgent student welfare issue that had to be dealt with before the end of the day. They established that a phone call needed to be made to the parents. Ben would usually make these calls himself but the assistant principal offered to make the call on his behalf so that he could go home for the weekend. After discussing the issue, the assistant principal began winding up their conversation. However, Ben found himself asking questions about a less urgent school matter. The assistant principal was clear and somewhat curt in her reply: 'I think that can wait until Monday.'

Ben felt annoyed that he had been cut off. However, later when he was driving home, he reflected on the fact that the matter could indeed wait until Monday. Ben was reminded of the important question we should all ask ourselves when facing our to-do list: Does it need to be done right now? Perhaps one way of organising our tasks could be along the lines of *must do* and *could do*. We might find that the things that we think must be done are actually fewer in number and therefore much more manageable than we had imagined.

We might also find that the tasks on our to-do list do not have to be done only by us. Revisiting our priorities in this way can prompt us to recognise where we have added to our sense of being time-poor by evoking an irreplaceability complex. We can forget that there are others, perhaps our colleagues or senior staff, who would be capable and willing to support us in completing the tasks on our to-do list. For each item on our to-do list, keeping it real therefore involves asking ourselves is there someone else who is in a better position to do this? Can I ask for help so that I can do one thing at a time?

In reflecting on his conversation with the assistant principal, Ben also realised that his colleague was respecting not only his own need to recharge on the weekends but also her own. She had done Ben a great service – in a few short words she had shown Ben that we all need to keep it real and only do what is possible and appropriate at the time. With these reflections, Ben started to take responsibility for reorganising his life so that he could rest well over the weekend and be grateful for the time off.

While we are busy writing lists and planning to get things done because we believe they will improve our future situation, we can miss what is needed of us right now. This scenario with Ben might prompt us to revisit our priorities and assess whether they relate to the future or now, and whether or not we are indispensable. Reflecting on this can bring us back to a more honest and grateful relationship with time.

Be grateful for the present

Ben's need to develop a healthier relationship with time also became obvious when he realised the impact his mistake about the excursion had on his students. This was a big wake-up call for Ben. He realised that something had to change. When Ben apologised to his students, he was acutely aware of many occasions when he had lacked presence and a capacity to be with them fully because of his busyness. At that moment, Ben looked over at Emanuel, a student who had come to Australia five years before as a refugee from Africa. The level of presence and state of being that Emanuel brought to nearly every class had struck Ben many times in the past. Emanuel often seemed more attentive than other students and gave his whole self to his work. Ben used to find himself wishing that all his students could have some of what Emanuel had, but now he was wishing this for himself.

In getting to know Emanuel, Ben was able to see that this student's whole approach to life was one of gratitude: gratitude for being alive when he could have been one of the hundreds in his village who were killed; gratitude for the chance he and his family had to settle in a relatively peaceful and prosperous country; and gratitude for the opportunity to go to school and gain an education. Of course, this isn't the outcome for all refugee students, as many are understandably crushed by their experiences and trauma. However, for those who are able to find gratitude, they can teach us so much about its power to help us be in the present moment. As Michael Brown (2010) says, 'Gratefulness is the one single marker we can depend on as an indicator of how present we are in our experience' (p. 10).

Ben felt ashamed that his own gratitude was severely lacking. He was caught in a trap of focusing on the time he didn't have. He was also so busy that he forgot to notice the things around him for which he could be grateful. This wake-up call made Ben determined to start each day and lesson by asking himself 'What am I grateful for?' as a way of keeping him in the present moment. He also resolved to ask this question whenever he felt overwhelmed by the busyness of his tasks. In this way, Emanuel became Ben's greatest teacher.

Feel abundant

We should never underestimate the power of saying the words *thank you* to grow a sense of abundance when we are feeling time-poor. Uttering these words gives us the ability to bring our attention back to the present and reminds us of what we can be grateful for in that moment. This is important when we feel time-poor, which generally has us feeling the opposite of abundant because we feel an absence or deficiency.

This is exactly how Ben had originally perceived his situation – a lack of time and energy. Now, by uttering thank you when he noticed the simple things in his life, like the smile of a student or the thoughtfulness of a cleaner, he felt a greater sense of what he did have and complained less about the things he didn't have. These words of thanks helped him notice what he had in abundance, rather than what had been taken away.

We can grow our sense of abundance by observing what we might have taken for granted. This can be highlighted by the attitude we bring to our tasks where we shift our thinking from what we *have* to do to what we are *able* to do (Nelson, 2020). Further inspired by Emanuel and his family, Ben noticed that he had been dominated by a sense of obligation and responsibility rather than treating the time he had preciously, as a gift. Because Emanuel had lived through many years of having much of what was precious ripped away from him, he had learned not to take anything for granted.

Ben started to write a list of all the things he had taken for granted about his job. He noted, for example, his physical capacity to work, his great colleagues, his inspiring students, his love of teaching and the views on the ride to work. He then decided to focus on being present and grateful for these things. Over time, this helped Ben be less flustered and overwhelmed by tedious tasks. It also infused the tasks he had long resented with gratitude for his feelings of abundance.

Summary

There is no doubt that urgent action is needed to curb the increasing time pressures faced by teachers. When we work in environments where we feel swamped by ever-growing expectations and where we never feel we get enough done, the suggestion of practising gratitude may seem to trivialise our plight or add to our to-do list. However, while we may not be able to control the unrealistic external expectations of our time, we can change our relationship with the time we have.

Gratitude for time helps us to more fully understand the nature of time and work with it rather than against it. A healthy perspective on time helps us to see that we are perhaps doing more harm than good if we try to multitask. When we are grateful for the time we have and stop ourselves from taking this time for granted, we can grow our sense of abundance and find joy in our tasks.

Put it into practice

As we have explored, it took time for Ben to grow his gratitude practice. Likewise, we are not suggesting that you implement each and every gratitude practice offered here immediately. Just taking up one or two gratitude practices at a time is very powerful and more achievable than trying to do too much at once.

- **Be grateful for time.** What are some of the ways you waste time or consider time your enemy? Looking at this honestly, how does this contribute to your sense of being time-poor? How can you plan your time more effectively and treat time like your friend?

- **Do one thing at a time.** Write a to-do list and practise doing one thing at a time, putting your whole attention to the present moment before moving on to the next activity. You might find that taking a deep breath can help you come back to the present more fully.

- **Keep it real.** Rewrite your to-do list through the lens of *must do* and *could do*. What are the things that can wait? Have you developed a sense of irreplaceability in any of your tasks? If so, how could you respectfully ask someone else to support you?

- **Be grateful for the present.** What does being present or in the moment look and feel like for you? Recall someone in your life who has this quality and try to discover how they developed it. What can you learn from them? Practise asking yourself many times a day, 'What am I grateful for?'.

- **Feel abundant.** Take note of three things that you have taken for granted recently in your role as a teacher. Reflect on how you could express more gratitude for these things. Examine your to-do list. Try to approach this from the perspective of what you are *able* to do rather than what you *have* to do. Do you feel a sense of abundance when you do this?

CHAPTER 2

Exhausted

It was the last week of first term. I'd had a rough night's sleep. Again. As I got dressed, I was haunted by last-minute preparations I needed to squeeze in before classes started. I kept telling myself: 'just put one foot in front of the other'. But I felt utterly exhausted, physically and emotionally.

Lisa, Year 8 mathematics and science teacher

An invitation

Do you ever feel so exhausted that you wonder if you can get through the next lesson, let alone the whole day or the rest of the term? Has this made you feel that things are beyond your control? Is your deep tiredness affecting you professionally and personally? Or maybe you are seeing colleagues like this and want to protect yourself before you reach this level of exhaustion or burnout?

With increasing demands on teachers' time, as well as the other challenges and pressures they face on a daily basis, exhaustion and stress are becoming a constant presence in teachers' lives. In this chapter we invite you to consider the crucial role that deep gratitude can play in helping to build resilience and improve wellbeing, particularly when feeling burnt-out or exhausted. We explore the life-enhancing power of giving and receiving inherent in deep gratitude and offer practices that are accessible and sustainable, even for exhausted teachers. We also consider the ways in which Lisa's small acts of gratitude, including gratitude to herself, bring about big effects.

Have you hit the wall?

Nearly all teachers feel exhausted and stressed at different times during their career. Often, they hit the wall at the end of term or at the end of the school year. There are various memes attesting to this with pictures of frazzled looking teachers and quotes such as 'There is no tired like end-of-year-teacher-tired'.

There is also an abundance of research in this area which demonstrates the impact of high levels of exhaustion and stress felt by many teachers. In Australian schools, for example, almost six in ten Australian teachers reported feeling quite a bit or a lot of stress in their jobs (Thomson & Hillman, 2019). The key stressors identified were those of rising workloads, obstructive student behaviour, increasing demands from stakeholders such as parents, line-managers and curriculum authorities, and a sense of being underappreciated and devalued as a profession more broadly.

As Madigan and Kim (2021) demonstrate, burnout and lack of job satisfaction play a significant role in predicting teachers' intentions to quit. Likewise, Thomson and Hillman (2019) observe that teachers who report experiencing a lot of stress at work are more likely to want to leave teaching within the next five years. Those teachers also experience lower levels of self-efficacy and wellbeing.

The detrimental effects of stress, burnout and emotional exhaustion do not just reside with the teacher. A study of 1102 primary school teachers and their students in Germany examined the association between teachers' emotional exhaustion and student achievement (Klusmann et al., 2016). For example, results revealed that teachers' emotional exhaustion was negatively related to students' mathematics achievement, highlighting the importance of teacher wellbeing for student learning. Put simply, student achievement suffers when teachers are exhausted.

Falecki and Mann (2020) also note that globally, teachers have the highest levels of work-related stress compared to other professions, citing the increasing burnout and attrition rates of teachers. As they observe, teacher stress impairs health, decreases motivation, self-confidence and self-esteem, and undermines personal relationships. These authors also report that as well as feeling exhausted, teachers can experience a sense of powerlessness and isolation, poor job satisfaction and perceive their work as meaningless. Falecki and Mann (2020) discuss the fact that teachers will become burnt out if their emotional, physical and mental exhaustion from excessive and prolonged stress is not addressed. The daily pressures of teaching, long working hours, an inability to switch off after work and poor work–life balance affect teachers' abilities to cope, their wellbeing and their potential to flourish.

The exhausted teacher

Along with her colleagues, Lisa had begun the year feeling optimistic, excited and energetic about her new posting and the year ahead. These positive feelings were boosted by a long, relaxing summer break and the welcoming, collegial conversations with other teachers in the week before the students returned. There were a number of new staff at the school, including Lisa, and a great deal of positivity in the air. Feeling fresh and well-rested, many of them had a lot to be grateful for. They shared happy snaps from the summer holidays and their hopes for the school year ahead. Lisa was looking forward to the opportunity this new role gave her to pursue her passion for making a difference and engaging students with new and innovative ways of teaching in her subject areas.

However, only ten weeks into the school year, Lisa was feeling emotionally, mentally and physically exhausted and unable to access the same level of optimism. She was overwhelmed with how much she had to do and couldn't get on top of things: preparing resources; writing learning plans for students with additional needs; making phone calls to parents and carers; designing rubrics and marking assessment tasks. At any given time, she might also have a line of students at her door wanting to catch up on work missed, asking questions about assessment tasks, complaining about their parents or whining about their friends. On top of this, her time seemed ill-spent lining up at the photocopier in the mornings, replacing the bottle in the office water cooler yet again and attending staff meetings on numerous afternoons.

Lisa's exhaustion was compounded by her feelings of failure and inadequacy. She compared herself to her colleagues who seemed to be coping better than her, even noticing the healthy, thoughtfully prepared lunches they brought to work. Lisa also noticed that she was more irritated by her students' behaviour and snapped at them impatiently. Sometimes, in the middle of the lesson, she found herself shrugging and thinking 'I just have nothing more to give'.

As a result of her overwhelm and stress, Lisa's hopeful start to the year and her gratitude for the opportunities it presented had completely faded. No matter how much she tried, she could not access the same positive emotions. Her self-confidence and self-esteem had plummeted. In her state of deep exhaustion, Lisa could not see how she was able to offer anything to anyone, let alone her students.

Gratitude. Seriously?

How could gratitude possibly help Lisa when she was so exhausted? All she felt like doing was curling up in bed and resting. Don't we run the risk of adding to Lisa's feelings of inadequacy by suggesting she take up deep gratitude practices when she is already unable to successfully complete her tasks? Teachers like Lisa may well think that a suggestion for gratitude means they are being asked to give even more. In situations like these, teachers need things that nurture them, not things that demand more of them.

Lisa knew that not only was she failing to cope with the pressures of the job but she was also failing to find any gratitude. Even if she thought gratitude was a good thing and would benefit her students, this simply added to her sense of despondency and stress since she was finding it impossible to access. As mentioned, she was already contrasting herself with her colleagues who seemed to be coping better or appeared grateful all the time. She was also comparing her present exhausted self with her more resilient and enthusiastic self from the beginning of the year.

Some may also question the wisdom of gratitude at these times as it can feel phoney or superficial. Indeed, there have been many critiques of gratitude when it is aligned with the positivity industry and the happiness agenda where people are coached to simply replace negative feelings with positive ones (Ecclestone & Hayes, 2019). This explains why gratitude can sometimes be confused with positive thinking. Positivity can seem like an easy way out of negative feelings such as overwhelm, stress, anger, frustration or anxiety: it can be more immediate and doesn't have to extend to others. At times when we are feeling exhausted, the pull towards positivity can be much stronger than the pull towards deep gratitude.

However, merely replacing negative feelings with positive ones is unsustainable. In fact, much has been discussed recently around toxic positivity: 'The unhealthy act of masking the reality of one's emotions by constantly engaging in forced positive affirmations' (Khatib, 2021, para. 3). In other words, by simply trying to replace negative thoughts with positive ones, we may be trying to numb our true feelings. We can adopt this as a strategy when we feel exhausted, but no matter how much we whip ourselves up into positivity, the exhausted feelings won't go away.

On another point, some might see the call for gratitude as an attempt to keep the status quo. A focus on gratitude might discourage teachers from advocating for better work conditions that would address teacher exhaustion in the first place.

Why gratitude?

As we explored in the Introduction, deep gratitude is about both giving *and* receiving. Being part of a giving profession such as teaching, most of us tend to be in giving mode rather than receiving mode. This why gratitude is especially important for teachers. If we can move into being more open to what we receive and feel grateful for this first, without forcing ourselves to give back immediately, we would find nourishment – something we're generally missing when we feel exhausted. This nourishment would benefit exhausted teachers like Lisa and teachers generally who want to build their resilience to avoid burnout.

As Barbara Fredrickson (2004) shows in her broaden and build theory, gratitude leads to individual transformation as people continually grow in 'an upward spiral toward optimal functioning and enhanced emotional well-being' (p. 153). As people become more grateful, they are 'more creative, knowledgeable, resilient, socially integrated, and healthy' and better at 'dealing with stress and adversity' (Fredrickson, 2004, p. 153). This is also demonstrated in recent developments in consciousness research and cognitive neuroscience. With regard to psychological health, for example, several studies have shown that having a grateful disposition offers some protection against depression and anxiety (Vernon et al., 2009) as well as stress and trauma (Vieselmeyer et al., 2017). Studies have also shown that gratitude leads to more refreshing sleep, improved heart health and immune system functioning, and reduces a range of other physical symptoms (Allen, 2018; Jackowska et al., 2016). Gratitude improves mood and lowers fatigue and may protect against burnout (Guan & Jepsen, 2020; Lanham et al., 2012). Research also shows that gratitude promotes positive reappraisal and healthy coping (Watkins, 2014; Wood et al., 2007).

Gratitude is also beneficial to the exhausted teacher when it is understood as deep gratitude and not merely positive thinking. The notion that gratitude is the same as positivity underscores one of the serious misuses of gratitude, expecting us to put a positive veneer over our negative thoughts and feelings. This might lead us to believe that gratitude is a simple fix to get us into a good mood and make our problems go away. Indeed, Howells (2012) demonstrates that a common misconception among teachers is that to be grateful, we also need to be positive. However, although gratitude can lead to positive feelings, it is a mistake to conflate positivity with gratitude and to treat them as if they are synonymous. Gratitude might boost other positive feelings, such as happiness, optimism, joy, pleasure and enthusiasm (Fredrickson, 2004) but these feelings are an outcome of our gratitude.

As you will explore in future chapters, a call for deep gratitude is never a call for showering endless praise on others or the systems we work in if there are problems that need to be addressed. Deep gratitude is a way for teachers to practise self-care and self-advocacy, especially in times of exhaustion or continued stress. Therefore, deep gratitude actually has an important role to play in helping us to advocate for change. It helps teachers to feel empowered and more resilient, which in turn means they are in a better position to challenge the status quo and promote the working conditions they deserve.

Distinguish between positivity and gratitude

Our first strategy in this chapter is to make a clear distinction between gratitude and positivity. This will help with the tendency teachers have to give themselves a hard time if they cannot muster up the strength to be bright, cheery and optimistic. Exhaustion can make us feel so depleted that it is hard to access such thinking. The last thing we want to do, especially at this time, is give ourselves further grief by feeling guilty or inadequate.

Deep gratitude and positive thinking are different and distinct ways of orienting ourselves to others and the world. One is highly relational and the other is highly individualised. Individually, we can think positively, try to look on the bright side and recall feelings of happiness. When we are thinking positively, there may be a reciprocal effect on others around us but we often find that positive thinking is possible without involving others. The same can be said for other actions that are often conflated with gratitude such as kindness, praise, applause or positive acknowledgement (Howells, 2012). Gratitude always involves the giving and receiving cycle and is therefore profoundly interpersonal (Emmons & Crumpler, 2000).

A helpful strategy for Lisa, and anyone else struggling to access gratitude or feeling a lack of authenticity, is to ask, 'Am I operating alone and trying to replace negative feelings with positive ones?' If the answer is yes, then it is likely that greater clarity is needed around what gratitude is in terms of the giving and receiving cycle. Instead of focusing on positivity or expecting herself to be positive about her exhausted state, Lisa could access deep gratitude by recognising that it involves connecting with what she receives.

Be open to receive

Instead of trying to feel positive about things she justifiably can't feel positive about, such as her poor working conditions, Lisa might open herself up to gratitude for what she receives from other things in her environment, such as caring colleagues or the view of a mountain from her classroom window. Therefore, an additional strategy to help us access gratitude when we are feeling exhausted is to notice what we receive from others and how we feel about the things we have been given. As Steindl-Rast (1984) reminds us, '… the circle of gratefulness is incomplete until the giver of the gift becomes the receiver' (p. 17). In her exhausted state, it would be helpful for Lisa to become the receiver.

Our research has shown that it's much easier for people to be in giving mode than receiving mode (Howells, 2021). This challenge is magnified in 'caring professions' such as teaching (Noddings, 2005), where people's identity and sense of self is bound up in what they give to others. Teachers are usually positioned as the givers of education, so for Lisa, receiving from others might seem counterintuitive. To be the receiver of another's help or gratitude not only calls for a change in the way teachers traditionally think about their role but also takes a certain vulnerability and humility. Yet, unless we welcome that help and replenish our own sense of gratitude, the gratitude we express to others might feel forced or inauthentic. Lisa was at a point where she felt like she had nothing left to give. By allowing herself to be in receiving mode, her situation was more likely to change for the better.

It was difficult, but Lisa needed to sit back and let others take on extra tasks so that she could lighten her load. This became apparent when she walked into her office which she shared with two other teachers and one asked how her morning had been. Lisa looked at her blankly and it quickly became obvious that she wasn't travelling well. Not for the first time, they recognised she was close to tears. Lisa's colleagues encouraged her to sit down and made her a cup of tea, laughing about their own lesson disasters that day, offering to share resources and more. Moreover, she received some sage advice: they encouraged her to see that she needed to sit back and let other staff help her out where they could. She also had the right to say no to additional duties and if she did so, she might actually be helping others who were also struggling to say no. Lisa's vulnerability in this moment helped her to receive from these colleagues and she was grateful for this.

This gratitude also helped Lisa to start to grow her awareness of what she was receiving in other areas of her work. She noticed the clean staffroom and appreciated the tireless efforts of the maintenance staff, the smiles that her students gave her, the lovely way a student was always there in the morning to open the door for her.

In receiving mode, this gratitude had a flow-on effect for her students. Research shows that when we look for and open ourselves up more to what we receive from our students, they feel more connected to us and more engaged (Howells, 2014). Over the following weeks, Lisa began taking the time to stop for a moment to savour these things, helping her feel calmer and more connected to those around her. She was also able to breathe a little easier. By receiving, Lisa became more aware of how others valued her, which in turn helped her transform the way she saw herself and increase her sense of self-worth.

Notice gifts

Once we are able to shift into receiving mode, we are also able to notice more of the gifts around us and appreciate them. For example, when we approach a colleague, rather than being fixated on our practical issues and how that colleague might resolve these we can reflect on what we receive from that relationship and how that relationship is a gift.

While exhaustion was the predominant state for Lisa, she was gradually able shift her attention to the gifts in her life. Rather than trying to force gratitude, she could focus on things such as the beautiful night sky or the car she loved driving to work. She could recognise the sense of awe, wonder and surprise these things brought her – the sense of giftedness that leads to gratitude.

There are many resources on how to access gratitude through this sense of appreciation. Those related to wellbeing include keeping a gratitude journal where, daily or weekly, you record five things you are grateful for. Research shows that this strategy alone assists people to feel more energetic, alive, awake and alert (Emmons & Smith, 2020). In another study, it was shown that writing a gratitude letter to different people for three consecutive weeks leads to greater life-satisfaction, decreased symptoms of anxiety and depression, fewer negative emotions, and better functioning in life more generally (Wong et al., 2018).

Further, as we explore in later chapters, although it could seem a stretch, we might ultimately see our challenges – even exhaustion – as gifts for what they teach us about ourselves. For example, we could be grateful for the opportunity exhaustion presents to learn more about what we value and how to set boundaries in terms of a work–life balance. As gratitude awakens us to a sense of giftedness, it can also bring our focus to the present and free us from worry about the past or the future. The joy and sense of calm that the present moment gives when we are in a state of deep gratitude has a generative power. As Emmons and Smith (2020) explore, gratitude is an affirmation of goodness, helping us to appreciate the inherent value of things and thus take less for granted. At the same time, it awakens us to the source of this goodness and so helps us to feel more connected.

Take action

Now that Lisa had been nourished by being open to what she received and noticed the gifts around her, she was more able to engage in the giving aspect of the gratitude cycle. She could now look at how she could give back in some way for what she had received. For example, greeting her students with her full attention and being would grow Lisa's gratitude and give her more energy to face the day. For Lisa, even in her exhausted state, she found it easier to act on her gratitude in relation to her students. Although she was always wanting to express her gratitude to them, this had been overshadowed by her exhaustion. She was now able to revise this by thanking them more genuinely for their patience when she wasn't fully prepared for the lessons and the lengths they went to support her when she left her reading glasses at home. She also made greater efforts to be more present to her students' individual needs during class time. This was all done with a spirit of gratitude – giving back out of acknowledgement for what she had received.

As mentioned in the Introduction, gratitude becomes deep when we act on our feelings of appreciation or thankfulness. Deep gratitude as an action moves us beyond being consumed by our feelings and, as Komter (2004) says, encompasses an imperative force 'that compels us to return the benefit we have received' (p. 201). When we express thanks to another, our gratitude reaches a deeper level because we externalise it and act on it. By taking action, we are creating movement or change, even in modest ways. Our being and doing amplify our gratitude and create a positive flow-on effect, even more powerful than our internal gratitude.

Take small steps

Once we have accessed the fortifying powers of gratitude, we might think it's important to feel grateful all the time to all people – this is not so! We need to remember the potential damage this pressure or sense of failure can do, especially to exhausted teachers. Rather than taking up that impossible task, we should ask 'what is one small step I can take to express my gratitude?'

As Lisa took more notice of the gifts she was receiving from her colleagues when she was feeling overwhelmed, she also took more notice of their exhaustion and stress. She could see the pressures of the term clearly taking a toll, evident in the pale faces and dark circles under the eyes of some of her colleagues. Rather than taking big acts of gratitude or trying to thank these teachers all the time, Lisa took small practical steps such as buying a packet of chocolate biscuits to share with her colleagues. She deliberately took time to ask her colleagues about their weekend and listened to their answers, consciously switching off from thinking about the next thing she had to do. She wrote a note to say thank you to another colleague who had shared some resources with her at the last minute. She smiled and stopped for a short chat as she held the door open for the cleaner. These small things made Lisa feel more energised and connected to her school community, which in itself grew her gratitude.

What made these acts of deep gratitude, rather than acts of kindness or obligation, was Lisa's attitude. She had been motivated by what she had received from her colleagues and acted with a heart of gratitude. As we will continue to explore, an important point is that Lisa wasn't expecting anything in return. Acts of gratitude are purely for the sake of giving, with no expectation of return or reciprocity. Small, achievable steps like these are an accessible way of acting on and externalising gratitude when we have low energy or feel defeated. Amazingly, when offered in authentic and meaningful ways, these small steps can transform relationships, staff cohesion and the whole school culture.

Give to yourself

A gratitude practice teachers might access when exhausted is one that is often overlooked: giving to self. Teachers tend to more naturally give to others, which makes giving to self a challenge for many. When teachers are overwhelmed by the complex and competing demands of their job, self-care or self-regard is often the first thing they overlook. This can be underpinned by the misguided belief that by sacrificing themselves and their needs, teachers will have more energy available for their students.

In the hope of keeping up, Lisa was regularly taking piles of student work home to mark and staying up late to prepare learning resources. She repeatedly turned down social engagements with her friends – usually a great source of joy and nurturing. Lisa started missing her gym class and her diet slipped as she grabbed takeaways on the way home from work, more frequently bought lunches from the school canteen and stopped stocking her own refrigerator as often. Her sleep was regularly disturbed as she woke through the night remembering a troubling conversation with a student or the additional tasks she needed to get done to prepare for class the next day. Unfortunately, by sacrificing our usual self-care routines as Lisa did, we do not increase the energy we have available for our students. On the contrary, our feelings of exhaustion multiply and we find ourselves spiralling into survival mode until the next school holidays afford us a decent break.

It is important to remember that we need to nurture ourselves and care for our own health and wellbeing. This might involve going for a swim, listening to music, a phone call with a friend, a romantic dinner or a massage. However, for teachers in an extreme situation such as Lisa's, these practices of self-gratitude often seem inaccessible. If this is the case, we can start with even smaller actions.

Another reason some teachers sacrifice themselves and their needs is because of a diminished sense of self-worth. When we are feeling burnt-out or despondent or have nothing left to give, we often view ourselves as failures professionally. This is why we suggest exhausted teachers attempt small, achievable acts of self-care. Giving to self helps us to acknowledge our inherent value and goodness and appreciate what we receive from ourselves. It encourages us to practice self-compassion and to recognise our inner beauty, skills, strengths and achievements, so that we value ourselves and can build our resilience.

To access this, Lisa could write a letter expressing gratitude to and for herself. She could thank herself for things she is proud of or her strengths in getting through difficult times or the qualities she admires most about herself. She could take regular, brief breaks throughout the day, taking a deep breath and giving thanks to her body, saying 'thank you for my lungs, for my heart, for my voice'. Even smiling can be a form of giving to self. Research shows that smiling lowers stress, reduces blood pressure and can help us live longer (Coles et al., 2019). A smile also brightens up the atmosphere around you and makes others more connected to you. They are then more likely to reach out to you, helping to draw you out of your isolation or your sense of being overwhelmed.

Remembering the importance of small steps, Lisa might deliberately turn off the work notifications on her phone and attend to her emails for a shorter period of time each evening. In doing this with a heart of gratitude, she could acknowledge that this gesture is a form of self-gratitude, an honest attempt to re-establish boundaries around her working life. Lisa might also focus on giving to herself by using gratitude to address her sleep deprivation. Sleep researchers have found that practising gratitude improves sleep quality and duration (Wood et al., 2009). If we are grateful before we go to sleep, we may be less likely to have worrying thoughts that disrupt our sleep (Digdon & Koble, 2011). Again, journaling might be a good practice to adopt – recording some things to be grateful for before going to bed.

With these small steps in place and reawakening the joy and nourishment her friends provide, Lisa might then feel confident to reach out and seek support and reconnect with her friends. Rather than the added stress of going out to socialise, Lisa might invite them to come to her; to bring supplies, cook dinner together, flop on the couch in front of a movie and accept her as she is, pyjamas and all. As gratitude is a deeply interpersonal practice, this could help her acknowledge her interdependence and embrace the giving and receiving cycle of deep gratitude.

Summary

Gratitude can often feel like the last thing we want to express when we are exhausted, especially deep gratitude, which involves taking action. However, moving from giving mode to receiving mode can be the most effective way to allow gratitude to replenish us. At these times, we need to ensure that it is gratitude we are trying to access, not simply attempting to feel positive. By noticing the gifts around us and taking up gratitude practices that open us to receiving these gifts on a physical, emotional and social level, we can indeed be lifted out of our exhaustion and gain back our sense of teacher effectiveness. However, we need to remember that this is a step-by-step process and sometimes the best way to give to ourselves is to be open to what we receive first. There is no harm in taking it slow: small or simple gestures of self-gratitude can have a profound effect on our wellbeing and do not have to take a lot of effort. This is the power of gratitude.

Put it into practice

Don't forget that we are not suggesting that you implement each and every gratitude practice offered here. Simply give one or two gratitude practices a go, and perhaps start with the ones that feel the most accessible. Again you might like to use your journal.

- **Distinguish between positivity and gratitude.** When you are trying to access gratitude while coping with exhaustion, is it actually gratitude you are trying to practice or are you trying to replace negative thinking with positive thinking? In your journal, make a note of the differences between these. Alternatively, discuss these differences with a colleague.
- **Be open to receive.** To what extent is it easier for you to be a giver than a receiver? Practise being open to receive by consciously taking in the goodness and kindness of others around you for a few moments every day.
- **Notice gifts.** When you are interacting with your colleagues, practise taking a moment to acknowledge what you receive from your relationship with them. Take in their goodness, their kindness, what they are teaching you and how they inspire you. If you haven't already done so, start a gratitude journal, where each day you note down at least five things you have received from others or the world around you.

- **Take action.** Write a list of all the things you are grateful for and try to feel that gratitude. Next to this list write up some actions you can take to express this.

- **Take small steps.** If you are moved to do so, express your gratitude to others in small ways that are manageable for you and meaningful to them. To access deep gratitude, practise giving just for the sake of giving, without wanting anything in return.

- **Give to yourself.** Find three ways in which you can nurture yourself over the coming week. Write a letter to yourself acknowledging your strengths and achievements. Practise gratitude before you go to sleep. Ask for help. Smile. Allow yourself to change your identity as a teacher to someone who both gives and receives.

CHAPTER 3

Perfectionism

My lesson plan was perfect. I had worked on it all weekend. But I failed to factor in the need to administer a bandage; the 3½ requests to go to the toilet; the remaining ½ that didn't quite make it; the foot that got stomped on; the kid who got punched and the subsequent tears. Not to mention how many times I had to raise my voice. No doubt the teacher next door could hear the chaos and I felt ashamed that this would further her opinion of me as a failure.

John, Year 2 teacher

An invitation

Do you spend hours planning a unit of work while your colleagues can do the same in half the time and apparently with far less stress? Do you ever find yourself procrastinating to avoid preparing lessons or writing reports in fear that you won't do a good enough job? Has your path to teaching been rocky because you struggled to submit assignments on time or beat yourself up because they were less than perfect?

When we are in perfectionist mode, we tend to set goals we cannot attain, along with impossibly high standards. We assume that if we do everything perfectly, we can avoid feelings of judgement, blame or shame. However, because we feel we can never measure up, we are constantly noticing our mistakes and worrying about letting others down. In this chapter we discover the role of gratitude in gaining a more realistic sense of what is achievable, so that we can orientate ourselves towards a more gentle and sustainable way of teaching.

We invite you to look at gratitude as a pathway out of perfectionism – something that plagues many teachers. We consider the story of John, who is suffering from this malaise of perfectionism. We navigate his journey through a series of deep gratitude practices that enable him to find hope in his teaching career.

Are we our own worst enemy?

The tyranny of perfectionism undermines many teachers, including their ability to practise deep gratitude. At times, we can tell ourselves that doing things perfectly is a virtue because we gain a reputation of 'getting everything right' and this can form part of our identity. However, aiming to do our best is not the same as perfectionism. Perfectionism is about trying to go beyond our best and never feeling good enough. The personal cost to us and those around us is immeasurable.

Perfectionism often starts when we are young and we carry it with us through school, to university and then into our careers. If that career happens to be teaching, perfectionism can show itself in a number of disabling ways. When we strive for perfection in teaching, and inevitably fail to meet our own unrealistic expectations, we can engage in dysfunctional behaviour like procrastination, self-aggrandisement and over-striving. Further, because we can't be perfect, we become our own worst enemy, disappointing ourselves and bringing on stress and negativity. Perfectionism can also create a vicious cycle, where we unintentionally inflict it on our students and colleagues. As Samfira and Paloş (2021) demonstrate in their analysis of perfectionist strivings in teachers, unhealthy perfectionism involves teachers being overly critical about their own and others' behaviour, intolerant of mistakes, obsessed with seeking approval and dominated by the evaluation and criticism of others.

Perfectionism contributes to high rates of burnout in teaching which, according to Rankin (2017), has reached epidemic proportions internationally. For example, in a study of eighty-two teachers in primary school settings in Konya, Turkey, it was found that participating teachers' perfectionist levels were above average and there was a significant relationship between perfectionist levels and burnout (Buyukbayraktar & Temiz, 2015). Similarly, the results of a substantial body of research by Mahmoodi-Shahrebabaki (2016), involving 276 Iranian English teachers, highlighted the impact of anxiety, exhaustion and perfectionism on the mental health of teachers, which combined led to high rates of burnout and teachers leaving the profession.

The 'perfect' teacher

John was an early career primary school teacher in his third year of teaching. He had recently won a permanent position at an elite private school teaching a Year 2 class. He had been fortunate to gain this position on the strength of his specialisation in science, technology, engineering and mathematics (STEM) subjects.

Before John started, he was extremely anxious about doing well, despite his success at university and the positive feedback he had received in his previous teaching position. He spent the preceding school holidays researching, collecting resources and planning lessons for his class. He also went to school earlier than required to set up his classroom, label books, put up inspirational posters, set up the first learning task for the year and so on. After a few sleepless nights and a mix of excitement, fear and responsibility, John met his students on day one already feeling tired.

Susan had been appointed as John's mentor. She was the only other Year 2 teacher at the school and taught in the classroom next door. Susan was much older, more experienced and had an excellent reputation after working at the school for fifteen years. Susan met with John regularly after school to provide feedback and advice. During these meetings, Susan and John also collaborated to develop units of work, compare assessment tasks and discuss student progress.

After just a few weeks of teaching, John was already finding the meetings with Susan stressful. Even though she praised his efforts and thanked him for all that he was able to share with her about teaching STEM, John wasn't able to take any of this in. Instead, he felt intimidated by what Susan achieved with her own students, her relative ease and her calm approach. All that John could see were his comparative failures. His way of dealing with this increasingly stressful situation was to spend even more time planning his lessons, marking books and preparing resources. Each morning he feared that his students, their parents or his mentor would notice the dark circles under his eyes. This situation brought John's imposter syndrome and sense of inadequacy to the fore, most evident in his self-talk on the way to school: 'Will I make it to the end of the day without someone realising that I actually have no idea what I am doing?'

Gratitude. Seriously?

It is almost impossible for gratitude to thrive when we are in perfectionist mode. By definition, perfectionism orientates us to what is not working, what we don't like and what we feel is missing. Gratitude orientates us to the opposite, to what is working, what we appreciate and what we have received.

We can see from John's story that perfectionist behaviour can play out in a variety of dysfunctional ways. It diminishes our self-regard, self-esteem and self-confidence, and can cause us to take everything personally or become paranoid. It can even become our persona, where we put ourselves down and constantly overcompensate to cover up mistakes while comparing ourselves to others and what we feel they've achieved. The last thing we want to do is ask others what they think we can do to improve, let alone be told how we could practise gratitude more fully.

Looking closer, we can see that John wasn't really measuring himself against Susan's expectations, he was measuring himself against his own, creating disappointment when he couldn't reach his own standards, which were unattainable. Disappointment in ourselves can make us sick and cause us to be in a constant cycle of stress and self-resentment. As we saw from John's inability to take in Susan's gratitude, our perfectionism means that there is no chance of alleviating our stress by being replenished through gratitude towards us.

There may well be a deeper reason why John's perfectionism made it difficult for him to reach into gratitude. Baumeister et al. (2001) did an extensive review on thousands of psychological studies to ascertain if there were any common underlying themes. They came up with a now famous theory known as 'Bad is stronger than good'. Their findings are summarised by Watkins and McCurrach (2016) where:

> *Generally speaking, bad events, bad comments, bad interactions, bad thoughts, and bad memories have a more powerful psychological impact on us than do good events. Because of this, it is easy for individuals to become overwhelmed by negative information. (pp. 28–29)*

This is why, generally speaking, no matter how much we try to focus on the good, bad things can easily derail us. When we put perfectionism into this picture, it becomes even more difficult because of the predisposition to judge our shortcomings. While we are striving for perfection, our tendency to orientate ourselves towards the bad is magnified, making it difficult to access gratitude.

Why gratitude?

An important theoretical concept can help us overcome this phenomenon – the 'Amplification theory of gratitude' proposed by Watkins (2014) and Watkins and McCurrach (2016). This theory is built on the hypothesis that if bad is stronger than good, we need to develop our psychological wellbeing to make the good stronger than the bad. This is where gratitude plays such a significant and crucial role. When we are grateful, we are not just thinking good thoughts, we are amplifying these thoughts with feelings of joy, optimism and hope – we are making the good stronger than the bad. As Watkins and McCurrach (2016) point out, just as an amplifier increases the volume of sound in a microphone, gratitude 'turns up the good in one's life' (p. 28). They also describe how gratitude may amplify one's awareness and interpretation of beneficial events and memories as well as the good in others.

It is important to note that we are not replacing the bad with the good here or ignoring our negative thoughts and feelings. John wouldn't be expected to automatically start thinking good things about himself. But if he could be grateful for what he has received in his life, in his situation at school, in his efforts and his general worthiness as a human being, there is greater capacity to amplify the good so the bad thoughts generated by his perfectionism do not take hold.

If we can find a way to access gratitude when we are realising our mistakes and shortcomings, we can foster a spirit of acceptance rather than a sense of fear and dread. Indeed, the words *gratitude* and *grace* come from the same derivative of the Latin word *gratia* meaning thankful. We can take this to mean that a person who is acting with grace, acts in gratitude. Similarly, a person with gratitude has grace – a much admired teacher quality.

Amplify the good

When we are caught in a cycle of imposter syndrome, measuring ourselves against others and beating ourselves up for being less than perfect, we tend not to accept or register the gratitude others express to us. This can also bring out the cynic in us, questioning the intention of the other person. As mentioned in the previous chapter, one of the first ways into gratitude is to open ourselves to what we give and receive. Gratitude lives and breathes in relationships. We can help amplify it most fully when we are able to connect with others, give to them, receive what they are giving us and accept this as acknowledgement of our good. Therefore, our first gratitude practice in this chapter is to amplify the good.

For John to access gratitude and move out of perfectionism, he needed to find a way to graciously accept the gratitude he was receiving from others, including Susan. He needed to notice and celebrate his achievements and accept the praise others gave to him, rather than berating himself over what he wasn't achieving. John could start by amplifying the good in just one relationship. This could be with a particular student, a colleague or even a parent. It is always best to start with something that is a little out of our comfort zone but not too much. Given his current feelings of inferiority, his mentor Susan might be too much of a challenge for John's gratitude practice for now. John might want to select a colleague teaching another year level, perhaps also an early-career teacher, to start noticing what he gives to and receives from this colleague. If John can amplify this good and the impact it has on himself and his colleagues, this might help alleviate the pressure he is feeling about not being perfect. The next step could be to apply the same principle to another relationship – perhaps with one of his students or eventually, even Susan. Each time John attends to the good in his relationship with others, he could slowly become less consumed by what he perceives as his shortcomings, or 'the bad', and amplify his sense of the good.

Practise humility

An additional way out of perfectionist tendencies is to recognise that an important pillar of our gratitude is humility. With humility we can accept that we are not perfect and that we need to embrace our mistakes and our flaws.

If haunted by perfectionism, one way to develop our humility would be to consider the consciously incompetent model developed by Curtiss and Warren (1973). If we apply this model to the teaching profession, we find that the beginning teacher often starts out feeling unconsciously incompetent. Alongside much of the non-teaching population, beginning teachers can assume that teaching will be easy or that they already have the skills needed because they went to school themselves. At this stage, unconscious incompetence means that teachers can be blissfully unaware of the difficulties and challenges of the job and therefore unlikely to feel anxiety or concern. It's only when beginning teachers actually start to teach that they realise it is more difficult than it seems.

Teachers then hopefully move into the consciously incompetent stage – a move that takes humility because they must recognise that they don't have all the skills required or that they aren't as good as they thought they were. To move into this stage also means that they will inevitably experience a range of emotions such as fear, anxiety and worry. It is also where imposter syndrome shines. For someone coming from a perfectionist mode like John, these feelings are magnified.

However, if we gracefully accept this process, we can then hopefully reach the next stage, which is consciously competent. Only after a number of years of teaching, and a willingness to learn from our inevitable mistakes, would it be natural for a teacher to move into the consciously competent stage where they can teach with confidence, but still feel the need to learn and grow and concentrate on the task at hand. The teacher would then ultimately move to the unconsciously competent stage, a stage of mastery where they feel totally at ease and teaching becomes second nature.

As an early-career teacher, John would ideally be sitting comfortably and humbly in the consciously incompetent stage in most areas of his profession. However, John's perfectionism caused him to try launching himself fully into the latter two stages of competency. By comparing himself to his mentor Susan, who was in the unconsciously competent stage in most of her activities, he was only seeing his inadequacies and putting unrealistic expectations on himself as an early-career teacher. John's constant striving for perfection reduced his capacity to acknowledge his incompetence in an honest and authentic way. He needed to find a way through this situation – to be able to give himself a break, readjust his expectations and feel safe immersing himself fully in conscious incompetence.

It is important to recognise that even an experienced teacher like Susan will continue to move backwards and forwards between these stages in various facets of their job. Susan's experience integrating STEM subjects into her classroom practice provides a good example. She actively and humbly re-entered the consciously incompetent stage to take guidance from John, who held greater proficiency in this domain.

Welcome feedback

Teachers, especially those who are stuck in perfectionist mode, are notoriously reluctant to seek feedback because they fear it will be negative. The idea of perfectionism locks us into the belief that there is a clearly defined notion of completeness and all we need to do is reach it. Once we have reached it, there is nothing else to strive for and therefore nothing to learn from experience, failure and feedback. However, research shows that when a person has a grateful attitude, they respond to feedback more positively and appreciatively, read written feedback more thoroughly, have greater optimism and seek support more willingly (Hemingway, 2011).

It wasn't until the day that a parent complained about John that things started to shift. It was only one parent and a minor complaint. However, because of John's perfectionist tendencies, he catastrophised the situation, spiralling into a complete sense of failure. This single complaint led him to conclude that teaching was not for him. It was only Term 2 and he was about to quit.

John's apparent confidence, as well as his STEM expertise, had fooled Susan into believing he was coping well. However, the day after the parent complaint she noticed the stress in his eyes. She met with him after school, asked how he was going and listened empathetically as the floodgates opened. John began to expose his vulnerability and Susan was surprised to learn that he was completely overwhelmed. The long hours of preparation, his inability to relax and switch-off on the weekends and the constant self-critique had eroded his confidence. He always felt he was underperforming and ashamed that he wasn't nearly as good as she was.

Susan again expressed how grateful she was for his efforts and all the work he had done on the STEM teaching materials, as well as the invaluable insights and fresh ideas he had shared with the school community. Susan told him she could see his potential to be a great educator if he could accept that perfection is not possible in teaching – there is always room for improvement. Susan helped him to reframe the parent's feedback as a learning opportunity. She also shared her own stories of parent complaints, as well as other mistakes and feedback she had learnt from that improved her practice over time.

In this scenario we can see the power of the giving and receiving elements of gratitude at play. The conversation John had with Susan enabled him to feel more accepting and trusting of his relationship with his mentor. In turn, Susan was able to express her gratitude by giving her full attention and wholeheartedness to John and through this she could sense his vulnerability. As a consequence, John began to receive her gratitude and felt buoyed by her positive reinforcement about his capacity as a teacher. It was as though he had heard it for the first time. He left school that day feeling hopeful. He opened himself up to the gift of feedback. From this point on, John was able to slowly become more comfortable, challenging himself to invite and welcome feedback from students, parents and colleagues. He also gradually began to develop his gratitude for some of his mistakes and see them as opportunities for change, learning and growth.

Lean into imperfection

In many ways the idea of perfection is essentially flawed. The ancient Japanese philosophy of *wabi-sabi* explains this beautifully. In tea ceremonies, the most highly valued bowls are those that have an uneven glaze or cracks or are shaped irregularly. These imperfections are part of the beauty of the object. This tradition speaks of taking pleasure in the imperfect, a celebration of the way things are, rather than the way they should be. This principle encourages us to be grateful for our imperfections.

A *wabi-sabi* philosophy can encourage teachers to engage in the reflective process by seeking out what isn't perfect in their practice and embracing it. There is always something we could have done differently, or an area in which we need to grow and change. This is especially relevant in teaching as there are so many events that will arise in the classroom that we simply cannot anticipate in our planning. We would go so far as to say that no lesson or learning program is ever perfect in its implementation, despite our preparation and experience. Indeed, as most teachers know, a simple case of flatulence has derailed many a perfect lesson plan!

John could apply the *wabi-sabi* philosophy by having gratitude for his imperfections, viewing them as part of being human and most importantly, as part of being a new teacher. This can be done anywhere, even in the middle of a busy, energetic classroom, for example, when we deviate from our lesson plan spontaneously because something unexpected happens. Looking forward, we can also reflect on how we might do things differently next time, focusing on what we've just learnt about our teaching practice, even though we know there might be more imperfections in the next class.

Practise self-gratitude

In the previous chapter, we explored the practice of giving to oneself. Here we extend this into the larger concept of self-gratitude: a practice that is particularly pertinent to moving out of perfectionist mode. Perfectionism is often a deeply ingrained habit that we can't recognise in ourselves. Indeed, an inherent part of perfectionism is that we hide our behaviour from ourselves and others. That is why it can go undetected for many years. It's also why it can continue unresolved – it just seems to be part of who we are. It often takes the care and attention of another to help us identify this trait in ourselves, deal with its detrimental effects and begin the journey of self-gratitude. This is very true for teachers, who are often accused of being perfectionists, to the point that it has become a reasonably common stereotype. As a result of his conversation with Susan, John was able to begin dealing with his perfectionist tendencies by first recognising their presence, their prominence in his self-talk and their destructive manifestation in these early stages of his teaching career.

Once the person who is in perfectionist mode begins to recognise how they beat themselves up whenever they make a mistake, they can aim to counter this behaviour by deliberately nurturing their self-gratitude. Self-gratitude, the practice of being grateful to ourselves, provides a powerful, alternative way of being (Howells, 2021). When you have self-gratitude, you have empathy and compassion for yourself and are nourished by opening yourself up to what you receive from others. You have greater appreciation for your inherent worth as a human being and spend time acknowledging your good points and being grateful for them. We focus on what we love about ourselves and all that we give and have been given. We accept our limitations and aim for the best without over striving. We celebrate the small gains, noticing and building on them.

Instead of looking at 100 per cent as the one and only target and berating ourselves for not getting there – as we tend to do when we are trying to be perfect – we can orientate ourselves from the 0 per cent starting point and express gratitude for what we have been able to achieve from this point. Such gratitude can increase our self-acceptance and enable us to amplify the good in ourselves and have more courage to address our mistakes (Howells, 2021).

Embrace discovery mode

Through self-gratitude we are also able to take on an alternative perspective to perfectionism and way of being which we call *discovery mode*. In discovery mode we are consciously and fearlessly looking for imperfections, for data that says we are off course. We see mistakes as a way to discover more about ourselves and others, looking for areas to improve and proactively re-adjusting our practice. Rather than feeling anxious and stressed about our imperfections, we feel light, energetic and motivated.

In discovery mode, we are kinder to ourselves. Instead of dwelling on the past with remorse and regret or dreading potential future mistakes, we are excited about what our challenges might teach us and how they can help us grow. We treat each day as a new day for which we can be grateful. In this process, it is important to notice the self-talk we use, in particular, the labels we give ourselves. When we apply the label *perfectionist* to ourselves, it implies that this is part of who we are – a fixed, stagnant disposition. It can be both a label that we give to ourselves and that others give to us. This can manifest in accusations of perfectionist teachers being overly controlling, rigid in their planning and reluctant to listen to feedback. Once burdened with that label it's difficult for teachers or others judging them to shift. However, we have seen many shift their way of orientating themselves to a much gentler and more accepting way, once they acquire the self-awareness and skills to do so and accept the perfection of imperfection. A significant step forward in discovery mode therefore is to recognise how to move beyond the label of 'perfectionist'.

We also need to recognise when we are applying a perfectionist perspective to our practices of gratitude. By being in discovery mode we can aim to avoid second-guessing ourselves and always wondering if we are getting it right. In discovery mode we would see that there is no such thing as perfect gratitude and no right or wrong way to feel grateful.

Further, if people or situations don't respond in the way we would like or expect them to, we might judge not only ourselves but gratitude itself. Perfectionist perspectives can have us doubting the impact of our gratitude practice. If we approach our feelings of gratitude from a perfectionist perspective, we can fall into the trap of judging ourselves if we don't feel grateful when we think we should or if we don't feel we have enough gratitude. The very notion of a practice means that we need to embrace discovery mode because it underscores the inevitability that we will not be perfect in our gratitude. This is why we call gratitude a practice. It is always a work in progress. We discover more about ourselves, the other person and gratitude itself, every time we practise it.

Summary

Talented young teachers like John are leaving the profession in droves because they feel burnt out. However, we believe that another, deeper reason is that many of them don't know how to manage their perfectionism. Many teachers enter the profession with unrealistic and impossibly high expectations of themselves and have not been educated in how to develop other ways of being. They may not accept the gratitude that others are giving them, and their negative self-talk and disappointment cause them to feel overwhelmed and undervalued.

In this chapter, we have explored the role of gratitude in addressing perfectionism. We have learnt that we can move away from a perfectionist perspective towards gratitude by noticing and amplifying the good in our teaching practice, embracing humility and inviting feedback from our colleagues and others. We have also investigated the benefits of leaning into imperfection and engaging in discovery mode as gratitude practices for teachers struggling with the challenges of perfectionism.

Put it into practice

It is again time to try and put these ideas into practice. Start by giving one or two a go and record your thinking in your gratitude journal. You might like to do this alongside a trusted colleague who has shown some interest in developing their own gratitude practice.

- **Amplify the good.** Before you go to sleep at night, write down your positive qualities, your strengths or anything you or others told you that you did well at school that day.
- **Practise humility.** Identify an area of your teaching practice where you can humbly step into the consciously incompetent stage. Reflect on some challenging feedback you have received from a student, parent or colleague and reframe this as an opportunity for growth.

- **Welcome feedback.** Actively seek feedback from a trusted colleague. Reflect on how you can be in a grateful space before, during and after receiving this feedback.

- **Lean into imperfection.** Notice when a lesson goes wrong and the role you played in this. Embrace this as an opportunity for learning. Discuss your mistakes with a trusted colleague, preferably one who has a sense of humour.

    Engage with the philosophy of *wabi-sabi*. Create or collect a powerful visual image of the principle of perfection in imperfection. For example, a broken bowl or weathered shell (or a picture of one) or anything else that helps you recognise the beauty of imperfection. Put this symbol where you will regularly see it.

- **Practise self-gratitude.** When you feel anxious from self-judgement or over-striving, ask yourself if you are looking at 100 per cent as the target and criticising yourself for not being there. Instead look at the 0 per cent and be grateful for what you have been able to achieve, the progress you have made.

- **Embrace discovery mode.** Notice your self-talk. Watch the labels you give yourself. Try to see your perfectionism as something that is not fixed but a perspective that you can change over time. In discovery mode, you can consciously notice and welcome mistakes as opportunities to grow and change.

CHAPTER 4

Angry students

It just felt yuck! To be spoken to like that in such a public way made me sick to the stomach. I took home his aggressive voice, his insults and his threats. They repeated in my mind when I tried to sleep. Senior staff had removed him from my class immediately and he won't be back for ten days. But he will be back.

Abigail, senior secondary humanities and social sciences teacher

An invitation

So far, we have focused mainly on the challenges relating to your internal state. Now we are moving on to chapters that help us navigate the everyday challenges which relate more directly to difficult relationships we might encounter with students, staff and parents. Difficult relationships can often be considered the most complex challenge for teachers.

Have you ever stood face-to-face with an angry student? Have you ever had a student's anger directed at you personally? What form did this anger take? Did it involve physical aggression, posturing, swearing or yelling? Or did you encounter their anger through gossip or online trolling? Have angry students deliberately tried to derail your lessons, humiliate you in front of your colleagues or students and undermine your authority? How did this make you feel?

Dealing with angry students is a serious problem for teachers. They can shatter our confidence, ruin our lessons, take our focus away from teaching and learning, and have a negative impact on our health and wellbeing. In some circumstances, they can also initiate a genuine fear for our safety.

In this chapter, we invite you to engage with a series of deep gratitude practices to help you gain back a sense of agency when dealing with angry students. We explore the story of Abigail and Noah, a teacher and student who are often at odds with one another. We follow Abigail's journey as she gradually finds ways to build her gratitude, resilience and inner strength to navigate one of the most difficult situations we face as teachers.

Do angry students make our task impossible?

When students are angry, they can be angry at the world, themselves, authority figures in general or the educational institutions they are forced to attend. According to Siegel (2014), children and adolescents can lose control more frequently because the human brain isn't fully mature until our early twenties. Adding to this, anger can erupt because of any combination of complex reasons such as sleep deprivation, hunger, underlying emotional agitation or trauma (Siegel, 2014).

Thus, while teachers are working incredibly hard to nurture the minds of future generations, they may also be simultaneously dealing with angry students. Indeed, teacher abuse has become more prevalent and many teaching practitioners are leaving the profession citing challenging behaviour as one of their concerns (Billett et al., 2019; Burns et al., 2020).

There is also mounting evidence that bullying and harassment by students are common occurrences in the day-to-day interactions of a teacher's workplace. For example, research by Qiao and Patterson (2021) involving over 200 teachers from China and the United States found that approximately one-third of participants had experienced student bullying. Meanwhile, Dolev-Cohen and Levkovich's 2020 study with 330 Israeli teachers highlights the growing prevalence of teachers being subjected to cyberbullying as well as the emotional distress for teachers who witness their colleagues being bullied online. Kõiv and Aia-Utsal (2021) further demonstrate that teacher-targeted bullying or victimisation, which involves being exposed repeatedly, over a long time, to verbal, non-verbal, indirect and physical abuse, can disempower us, undermine our confidence, have a negative impact on our mental health and destabilise our attempts to nurture productive learning environments. As a result, many teachers can struggle to feel respected professionally and this has a detrimental effect on their self-efficacy and wellbeing.

The rate of student suspensions, exclusions or expulsions, resulting from aggressive or violent behaviour towards teachers, is also on the rise (Hemphill et al., 2017). Suspensions might offer a short-term solution but the long-term costs to the student, the community and overall student engagement, are potentially very high. As Hemphill et al. (2017) demonstrate, students can become alienated from school, given 'suspension-status' by their peers or even become swept along in the 'school-to-prison pipeline'.

Teachers around the world are looking for a better way to help these students, and themselves, in managing this situation. The answer clearly doesn't lie in removing angry students from the classroom. However, the fallout from their ongoing presence can make our task seem impossible.

The angry student

Abigail had twelve years of experience teaching in educationally and socio-economically disadvantaged schools and was armed with a suite of tried-and-tested behaviour management techniques. For the first time in all these years, Abigail began to question her effectiveness as a teacher because she couldn't cope with being repeatedly verbally attacked by Noah. She was trying her best to manage this situation while juggling the other demands of her teaching role, including a busy classroom with a large cohort of disadvantaged students, many of whom had come to the school with a traumatic background. The hopelessness and despair Abigail was feeling about this situation was spilling out to other areas of her life and pervading her relationships with her children and her partner.

Noah was a tall, overweight and angry teenager. He would deliberately position himself between Abigail and where he knew she wanted to go; he would glare at her for no apparent reason; he would turn up to lessons late and swagger across the classroom to chat to a friend; he would taunt Abigail, encouraging other students to question her ability and undermine her lesson. If Abigail challenged Noah, he would lash out at her: 'You stupid cow!', 'How can you be a teacher when you're such an idiot?', 'What would you know with your pretty little life?' Every time it happened it would shake Abigail to the core. It felt like Noah was using her as an emotional punching bag. On her drive to work, Abigail began to feel physically ill when she thought of herself in the same room as Noah.

Because these angry outbursts happened in front of other students, Abigail was compelled by the school to set an example and have senior staff remove Noah from the class. More often than not this led to Noah being suspended from school for a number of days. The situation was made worse for Abigail because she thought she had made every attempt to understand Noah. She had read the extensive notes on his background. Noah had witnessed horrific domestic violence perpetrated by his father. His father was now in prison and his mother had substance abuse issues. Knowing this background, Abigail made excuses for his behaviour when questioned by senior staff. She often encouraged them to go light on his suspensions because school was clearly better than home. As a result, Noah's behaviour appeared to go unchallenged at times and he was invited to come back to school after every incident. As the year progressed, Abigail realised that her actions gave Noah licence to publicly shame and undermine women, and she felt implicated in perpetuating a cycle of misogyny.

While Abigail's experience is an extreme one, it is not as uncommon as we might think. For example, in a recent survey of 560 Australian teachers, over 70 per cent indicated they had been bullied or harassed by a student (Billett et al., 2019). This behaviour most commonly took the form of verbal aggression including swearing, yelling and disparaging verbal comments. These teachers also reported smaller, but still significant, rates of physical violence including being hit or punched by a student (10 per cent), damage to personal property (12.5 per cent) and having a student stand over them or invade their personal space (16.6 per cent; Billett et al., 2019).

The rising statistics on students coming to school with traumatic backgrounds are also telling. For example, in the United States, 26 per cent of children witnessed or experienced a traumatic event before they turned four (National Center for Mental Health Promotion and Youth Violence Prevention, 2012). Research on trauma-informed teaching practices has shown us that students with trauma backgrounds are more likely to have unpredictable outbursts in classrooms, including uncontrollable anger (Australian Childhood Foundation, 2020). Our job becomes desperately difficult when we are expected to manage the competing demands in our classrooms while also dealing with increasing numbers of traumatised students.

Gratitude. Seriously?

To speak of gratitude as a strategy for dealing with angry students might sound completely unrealistic. Often, the last thing we want to do when we find ourselves faced with anyone's anger is to try to access, feel or express gratitude.

As already mentioned, a common misconception is that we need to feel grateful all the time (Howells, 2012). Once teachers grasp the value of gratitude in less challenging contexts, they can feel downhearted or defeated if they can't feel gratitude when things are more complex. As you can imagine, it would be unreasonable to expect Abigail to feel grateful in this situation with Noah, particularly when he was verbally abusing her. Moreover, busy teachers, who have so many competing demands to address including those of the angry students in the room, can't possibly access gratitude as a constant, pervading emotion.

You wouldn't blame someone in Abigail's situation for asking: how on earth could gratitude make this situation better? Indeed, her situation underscores some of the dilemmas of applying gratitude in complex school environments. If Abigail tried to go straight to gratitude for having an angry student like Noah in her classroom, it's likely she would feel inauthentic or even more depleted.

We also face the ever-pervasive problem of thinking that a call for gratitude equates with accepting the status quo. Would a recommendation for gratitude be letting Noah off the hook and accepting his angry behaviour? We are reminded that Abigail was uncomfortable about perpetuating a cycle of misogyny by allowing Noah to treat women poorly because of his emotions, circumstances and background.

This cycle still needs to be redressed on a systemic level beyond Abigail's story. For example, there is perhaps a poorly resourced family and child protection system that struggles to help students like Noah; likewise, an education system relying on suspensions to deal with aggressive behaviour despite the ineffectiveness of this strategy. Again, a call for gratitude might be seen as a way of sweeping these significant problems under the carpet.

Why gratitude?

Abigail needed an authentic way into gratitude which did not involve ignoring Noah's behaviour or the systemic problems that led to this situation in the first place. This is obviously different to accepting things as they are and hoping that problems such as angry students will go away over time. We need to find areas where we can make a difference and grow our hope and optimism by focusing on these areas.

The dimension of deep gratitude that has the most significance here is the 'inner attitude'. When we pay attention to this, we realise why gratitude is important. Our inner attitude sits behind and greatly influences our thoughts, emotions, actions, physicality, beliefs and values (Howells, 2012; 2021). Whether we are conscious of it or not, we always have an inner attitude of some kind and this influences many other aspects of ourselves. It is not something we can switch on or off when we please. By attending to our inner attitude we are prompted to look within ourselves rather than blaming the external situation as the sole reason for our state of being. We can make changes in areas that we can change – within us. Based on the adage of self-efficacy, 'For things to change, first I must change', we advocate that if we focus on our inner attitude of gratitude, we are focusing on an area of ourselves that we can change, despite what is going on around us. This enables teachers in situations like Abigail's to gain a greater sense of agency and empowerment. In time, they might also begin to cultivate the energy required to advocate for the systemic changes needed.

As we noted in Chapter 1, 'we teach who we are' (Palmer, 2017, p. 10). Palmer goes on to state: 'good teaching cannot be reduced to technique; good teaching comes from the identity and integrity of the teacher' (2017, p. 10). If the teacher focuses on their inner attitude, they are able to develop this identity and integrity in a conscious way, without needing to feel grateful all the time.

Cultivate a state of preparedness

The importance of gratitude as an inner attitude is captured in the notion of a *state of preparedness* (Howells, 2012; also Howells, 2018; Howells, 2021; Howells & Cumming, 2012; Howells et al., 2017). This stands in contrast with our traditional notion of teacher 'preparedness' which is usually associated with the organisation and planning of things such as curriculum content, teaching resources and strategies, assessment tasks and student activities. Deep gratitude asks us to prepare the state of being that we bring to teaching.

To practise a state of preparedness we find a moment to imagine our day ahead and attempt to approach this with an inner attitude of gratitude. A state of preparedness works not by focusing on gratitude in the midst of our activities – when we are distracted or facing the challenges of angry students – but by filling our inner attitude with gratitude before the day begins, or before going into a classroom, or before we are about to interact with someone. The inner attitude that we have when we wake up in the morning and when we are driving, cycling or walking to work, will have an impact on the outcomes of the activities during the day. We set the tone, the atmosphere – both inside and outside ourselves – for what is about to take place.

While Abigail might not be able to access gratitude for Noah directly, she could still try to start her day with a state of preparedness. For example, she could turn her attention to her gratitude for her own children, her partner, her colleagues or students she has a positive relationship with. Abigail could think of the gifts she receives from each of these connections. She could also access self-gratitude by recognising the strengths and achievements she brings to her classroom and her colleagues as an experienced teacher.

Another reason we should try to cultivate our state of preparedness is that our inner attitude impacts our students from the moment we enter the classroom or school. It can make a world of difference to our words or actions and is at the core of who we are as teachers. If we prepare our inner attitude before we teach, before we get to school, we can have a considerable influence on our ability to foster positive relationships with our students. While this may not be immediately obvious with students like Noah, the effect our inner attitude can have on others helps to build a sense of connectedness and community in our classrooms, which can buoy us at difficult times.

Reflect on success

One of the most powerful ways for teachers to cultivate a state of preparedness is to deliberately take time to reflect. Reflection isn't just about looking at our failures but also at our strengths as an educator. It's about digging deeper, identifying the good choices we have made throughout our career and articulating our gratitude for these. This reflection enables us to build our sense of self, affirm our teaching identity and deal with the inevitable difficulties of our profession so they don't crush us and so that we can feel less despondent.

As Abigail desperately tried to navigate this low point in her career, she reached out to a trusted colleague who encouraged Abigail to reflect on the successes of her past teaching experiences. In conversation with this colleague, Abigail was able to express gratitude for her own commitment to the teaching profession and her other students, as well as the fact that she was at least turning up to school every day. Reflecting like this helped to underscore the hope, empathy, selflessness and compassion that she, like most teachers, brought to her practice. Indeed, Abigail started to see that this commitment was perhaps the very reason she experienced such a deep sense of failure in relation to her inability to support and connect with Noah.

Starting to feel more resilient after this conversation with her colleague, Abigail continued to reflect on the goals she had kicked so far in her career by taking out the pile of home-group photos she had collected over twelve years. She could easily identify so many students that she had established a deep connection with. She remembered their stories and the ways she had helped to transform their learning opportunities. By retracing her teaching journey through photos, Abigail found self-gratitude for her ever-strengthening resolve to build relationships with students. She was also able to congratulate herself for the efforts she had made to open doors for countless students over the years. Even though Abigail knew she had failed to do this with Noah, by explicitly identifying and validating her past successes with other students, she was more easily able to access gratitude as an inner attitude.

We might also express our gratitude for the ways our actions as teachers will live on, some of which we may never know or might experience much later. In her book, *Teaching Outside the Box* (2015), LouAnne Johnson captures this in her story of a person who ran a private detective agency and was asked about the most common reason people hire private detectives. We might think that it would be to investigate people who are having affairs, but no. After interviewing over 150 detectives in this agency, the most common request was to find a former teacher to thank them!

Accept limitations

A further strategy for accessing deep gratitude is to be realistic about the circumstances we are working in and the accompanying constraints of our job. As teachers, we need to recognise that there are real barriers outside of our control that make it difficult to connect with some students. For example, Noah's background of abuse and neglect meant that it was difficult for anyone in authority to establish a trusting relationship with him, especially over the course of a single year. Noah's case notes also indicated that he had witnessed misogynistic violence on a number of occasions, which contributed to normalising his hatred and disregard of women. Further, while Abigail had undertaken a professional learning course on working with students with traumatic backgrounds, it had only been a two-week seminar. Understandably, she was no expert.

In recognising the limitations of the broader educational system and our classroom context, we can find a way not to be so devastated when confronted with angry students, and what might feel like our failure to reach them. That is, we can practise self-gratitude simply by giving ourselves a break for not being superheroes. At the same time, we can also be grateful for areas in which we do have some agency and where we do take action.

Abigail practised self-gratitude by honouring the fact that the attacks she was subjected to were simply not okay. She was not prepared to accept them and put herself, her health and ultimately her family, second to Noah.

Receive from others

We again consider how being grateful for what we receive from others can support teachers dealing with the daily problems embedded in their work. For Abigail, this involved turning her attention to what she received from her colleagues. Driving to work, she reflected on the gratitude she felt for the support from a colleague, Sam, who taught in the classroom next to her. After explaining her situation, Sam made a commitment not to leave his post if he knew Noah was in Abigail's class. He even did his marking in his classroom to accommodate this, rather than in the quiet of his office.

In addition, the first time Noah verbally attacked Abigail, her principal, Joan, sat with her while she cried in her office. Abigail was very grateful for Joan's care and thoughtfulness: she arranged for someone to cover Abigail's classes, touched base with her partner to make sure she had support when she got home and collected her bag so she would not need to re-enter the classroom that day. Over time, Joan noticed Abigail had become more and more sleep deprived and riddled with doubt about her ability as a teacher and she caringly encouraged Abigail to take a week of paid stress leave. Abigail was grateful that this time enabled her to access a counsellor, particularly as she had worked in other schools where this kind of support had not been offered. This counsellor reassured Abigail by observing that her task of dealing with this angry student was impossible, remarking: 'You're trying to fight a bushfire with a garden hose.'

When she returned to work, Abigail consciously held on to the gratitude she felt for her supportive and understanding colleagues. This grew her capacity to push through the dread she felt about having to interact with

Noah in the day ahead. The conscious attention she paid to her gratitude for her colleagues on a regular basis grew her sense of resilience and capacity to deal with the difficult situation with Noah. Abigail's gratitude also reinvigorated her commitment to nurture her collegial relationships. In addition, Abigail had a fresh perspective on her profession as a whole. After teaching for so long, Abigail had found herself at risk of becoming jaded, but this experience underscored the awesomeness of the people she worked alongside and the lengths that they went to. Once again, she was proud to be a part of this profession.

Find gratitude for angry students

We have deliberately left this gratitude practice until last because it is often the most difficult. As we have discussed, to access and express gratitude to those who cause us harm and make us feel unsafe at work, is often, understandably, beyond our reach. However, we offer this strategy for those who might see themselves as ready for a next step in that direction.

By consciously filling herself with gratitude in other areas of her life, Abigail might begin to feel resilient enough to look for gratitude for something in Noah and practise holding this in her inner attitude before interacting with him. This would mean that Abigail would go beyond just trying to find something positive to what she had received from him that could be considered a gift. This is what would make it a gratitude practice. Abigail started by thinking about how much Noah's resilience inspired her because she knew how difficult life was for him. She grew her gratitude for the courage and tenacity Noah showed in getting out of bed in the morning despite his difficult situation at home. Eventually, Abigail was also grateful for the opportunities this situation gave her to instigate deep reflection, as well as personal and professional growth.

The next step might be for Abigail to express this gratitude to Noah in some way, although at this stage, that felt like crossing a chasm she wasn't quite ready for. However, when we are ready to find and develop an inner attitude of gratitude towards angry students, even when it is unarticulated, they might still feel our gratitude. It is important that our gratitude is sincere, heartfelt and coming from a sense of giftedness, because students with trauma backgrounds, like Noah, often have their radar up to detect any falsity and can feel the difference between words of thanks that are real and those that are not. As Howells (2012) discusses, 'Students orient themselves to where they feel valued and where there is trust (Howells,

2012, p. 6). If they can feel the authenticity of our gratitude because it comes from our inner attitude, over time they are more likely to feel this trust. Of course, with some students we have greater success in this than with others.

Summary

Abigail might still have felt that she had failed to reach Noah or fully recover from the painful memories of his angry outbursts. However, there were a number of gratitude practices that worked for her – identifying her gratitude for the success she had in connecting with other students in her classrooms; being kind to herself by recognising the limitations of her expertise in dealing with students like Noah; and acknowledging the very real constraints of the education system she worked in.

Abigail also practised gratitude by identifying the support that was available to her. In doing this, she was able to recognise the calibre of individuals she worked alongside, which in turn renewed her commitment to nurture these collegial relationships. Finally, although she did not express it to Noah directly, Abigail was eventually able to identify things she could be grateful for in her angry student. In accessing these gratitude practices Abigail was able to navigate this difficult moment in her career and move forward.

Put it into practice

Have a go at one or two of these gratitude practices, perhaps starting with those that feel most comfortable. Then try to challenge yourself by attempting one that pushes you slightly outside of your comfort zone. You might like to talk about your reflections with a friend or colleague and record your ideas in your gratitude journal.

- **Cultivate a state of preparedness.** What is your usual routine when you are getting ready for school? Identify a quiet moment in this routine, perhaps while you are drinking your morning coffee, having a shower or driving to work. Reflect on what you are grateful for about the day ahead.

- **Reflect on success.** How have you positively influenced and connected with individual students in your classrooms? If you have them, pull out past class photos or yearbooks or cards, emails or letters written by students. Make a point of identifying one golden moment in your relationships with students every day for ten days. Write them down. Share them with a friend or a colleague.

- **Accept limitations.** What are the limitations of the context you are working in? Are there ways you can give yourself a break for not overcoming all the obstacles in our profession? Be kind to yourself.

- **Receive from others.** Identify another teacher, past or present, who you are grateful for. What have you received from them? How have they shaped you as an educator and supported you in your practice? Find a way to express your gratitude towards this teacher.

- **Find gratitude for angry students.** If you are ready, identify a student, past or present, who you find difficult or consider angry. Try to acknowledge something that you are grateful for about this individual. Try to go beyond praise and acknowledge what you have received from them. If you feel comfortable doing so, share some of this with them.

CHAPTER 5

Toxic staff relationships

I was new to the school. In just a few months, Martin, a teacher who had been there for twenty years, had placed me firmly in the out-group. When I walked into the staffroom, Martin and his mates would stop talking or change the subject. When I shared my ideas in staff meetings, I was met with scepticism and a scoff from this group of teachers. I felt excluded, belittled and lonely.

Hayley, secondary arts teacher

An invitation

Have you ever sat in a staffroom and felt a negative vibe from some of those gathered there for lunch? Do you sometimes find yourself avoiding the staffroom altogether because of gossiping and backbiting? Have you ever walked in on a group of colleagues chatting, only for them to go silent when you enter the room? Does navigating staff relationships take up too much of your productive and creative energy?

Like angry students, toxic staff relationships are detrimental to our effectiveness as teachers and undermine our overall job satisfaction, health and wellbeing. Our collegial relationships have a significant impact on our capacity to do our job well. If these relationships are unsupportive, competitive or destructive, we can often find ourselves starting to resent getting up and going to work.

In this chapter, we discuss how collegial conflict between Hayley and Martin created an unpleasant teaching and learning environment not only for them but for students and other staff. However, we also learn about some straightforward gratitude practices Hayley managed to put in place that respectfully initiate a way forward and eventually build a more positive connection with Martin.

Can collegial conflict make us less effective?

Teachers feel disappointed when they are treated with a lack of collegial fairness and respect. Underpinning this treatment can be any number of factors. Teachers can develop grudges with other teachers over seemingly minor issues such as the 'correct' way for students to line up before class or what constitutes acceptable shades of navy for the school uniform. Teachers can judge other teachers for supposed misdemeanours such as taking too much sick leave, appearing to slack off in collaborative planning teams, leaving staff meetings early or turning up late for their duties. Collegial resentment can arise if teachers believe they have been given more than their fair share of the difficult cohort of students or the less popular specialist subjects. They might also be offended if they think the teacher next door has access to more resources than them such as teacher aide support, time with the principal, extra stationery, desk space, even master keys!

Difficult relationships between teachers are further compounded by the increasingly competitive demands of the role. Teachers are often compared to other teachers by external measures of teacher quality such as professional standards and regulatory bodies (Pachler & Broady, 2022). They are encouraged to compete for permanent and promoted positions and for transfers into easy-to-staff or out of hard-to-staff schools. Even the nitty gritty of timetabling can put a strain on collegiality as teachers vie for the easy grade or student cohort or less yard duties and more non-instructional time. Meanwhile, a growing consumer mentality in education means that parents and carers might try to 'teacher-shop' and students can create popularity contests through websites such as 'Rate My Teachers' (Rate My Teachers, n.d.).

When teachers' grudges lead to toxic staff relationships, they can sabotage the school culture. If staff are gossiping and backbiting or competing with each other, it becomes very hard to focus on teaching and learning. This is amplified when there is no clear, shared sense of purpose among staff and an absence of trust and honest dialogue. More can go on behind closed doors, or behind people's backs, with issues being discussed in the unofficial 'meeting-after-the-meeting'.

Workplace bullying can also abound. Taylor (2021) characterises this as repeated acts or verbal comments made to the victim as a way of controlling and demonstrating power over them. As Taylor suggests, teacher-on-teacher bullying can be sly, difficult to address, and a taboo topic of discussion in many schools, compounding the negative impact for the victim. Indeed, Kleinheksel and Geisel (2019) found, in their survey of 324 public school teachers in Michigan, employers are often reluctant to recognise, correct or prevent workplace bullying when it falls short of illegal harassment. As a result, targets can feel victimised a second time by the lack of organisational policies addressing such abuse.

In their examination of workplace bullying among teachers, Bernstein and Batchelor (2022) also reveal how a school environment characterised by excessive demands, ever increasing workloads and a lack of supportive resources can make collegial conflict worse. Such an environment fosters stress, anger, frustration and aggression, increasing the perpetration of bullying acts as teachers turn on one another (Bernstein & Batchelor, 2022). In addition, Han (2021) demonstrates that when gossip amongst teachers is underpinned by jealousy, envy, unethical behaviour, vanity and aimlessness it has the potential to undermine the organisational function of schools.

Sinha and Yadav (2017) and Bernotaite and Malinauskiene (2017) also note the harmful effects of prolonged humiliation, excessive monitoring, deliberate undermining of work and belittlement in schools which result in anxiety, depression, occupational burnout, psychological distress and cardiovascular disease. Bernstein and Batchelor (2022) likewise indicate that the aftermath of bullying can include manifesting feelings of incompetence and emotional exhaustion, leading to teachers engaging in withdrawal behaviour and expressing an increased desire to leave the profession. Productivity, commitment, performance and job satisfaction are inhibited, staff absenteeism increases and the experience of workplace bullying may cause teachers to leave the profession (Jacobs & de Wet, 2018; Sinha & Yadav, 2017).

Of course, toxic staff relationships are inevitably influenced by the broader education system within which we work, as well as the hierarchies and political landscapes that go beyond the school grounds. However, as stated in the Introduction, while we acknowledge the real impact of these systemic impositions, our purpose is not to examine them in detail. Instead, the gratitude practices offered in this chapter focus on enabling teachers to take greater agency and build their capacity to change the things they can change, and support teachers like Hayley who are caught up in damaging relational dynamics at work.

A toxic staff relationship

Hayley had held short-term casual contracts up to this point. She was excited about her first permanent position which was at a regional district school, making a courageous move to the remote community far from her friends and family. She was motivated to see out her two-year contract at the school, knowing the experience would help her compete for a job closer to home. Having enjoyed the camaraderie of her first school, she felt confident about the move. However, after only a few months, Hayley started to see the job as a prison sentence and she began to count down the days until she could get a transfer.

Hayley's main problem was the conflict she had with Martin, a teacher with twenty years of experience, all at that school. Martin was deeply cynical of new teachers like Hayley, especially those who were young, seemed to have endless amounts of energy and didn't have family commitments. From his perspective, they came with a superhero mentality, seeking to 'fix' the students and the school culture. He was tired of them volunteering for additional duties, developing exciting and highly visible projects, attending extra committee meetings after school and ingratiating themselves with the principal. To Martin, these teachers were opportunists, using the school community to get ahead and pad out their resumes before moving back to the city – which they usually did after a couple of years.

Martin's behaviour towards Hayley made her feel isolated and lonely. He would regularly gather other teachers around him in the corner of the staffroom and didn't hide the fact that he was gossiping about her. He also seemed to make sure Hayley knew about their social gatherings after school that she hadn't been invited to. Hayley had even overheard Martin criticising her for her city clothes and city ways.

The tension and negative feelings between Hayley and Martin were obvious to everyone. Hayley started to avoid Martin whenever she could and when she did cross paths with him, found it hard to make eye contact or greet him. Martin only spoke to Hayley when he had to, answered her questions perfunctorily and smiled and nodded vaguely at the seemingly correct times. He was courteous enough to maintain his nice guy image, but accepting Hayley and actively including her seemed to be too much for him.

The vitality Hayley brought to her new position was dwindling as she struggled to develop her identity as an effective teacher. She started to feel despondent about ideas she previously had about bringing innovative practices to her classroom and suffered under the weight of loneliness and social isolation. All of this was to the detriment of her teaching, student outcomes and commitment to the profession.

Gratitude. Seriously?

How might teachers like Hayley access gratitude when they feel the exact opposite towards those who are causing such grief? Surely it would be best for Hayley to avoid Martin whenever possible and grin and bear it until her two-year contract ended? Indeed, when we feel we are being wronged by someone, we tend to wait until they change their behaviour rather than addressing the situation ourselves. We might also be waiting for them to recognise the damage they have caused us and to finally come to apologise or mend their ways. To be grateful when we feel resentful can seem like we are condoning disrespectful or unacceptable behaviour.

We may be well aware that gratitude is important for creating a positive school environment. However, it is often the case that it is almost impossible to practise gratitude in the midst of difficult relationships that have led to resentment (Howells, 2021). While there is resentment there can be no gratitude – each cancels the other out (Roberts, 2004). Even in situations where we want to express gratitude to someone we will find it hard to do so if we are holding a grudge from the past (Howells, 2021). This can leave us feeling ashamed that we cannot be grateful when we think we should be or that gratitude itself is an unattainable state. We could also aim to identify why we would want to practise gratitude in the midst of resentment. In this case, Hayley could ask what would be the advantage of her trying to access her gratitude?

Why gratitude?

We need to emphasise from the start that we are not expecting Hayley, or any other teacher who is experiencing such collegial conflict, to jump straight into gratitude for the person who is causing grief. As the rest of this chapter demonstrates, if we want to let go of our resentment, we can start by taking small steps in the form of specific gratitude practices. These steps may initially involve finding gratitude where we can find it.

An important reason to try to access gratitude, even in the midst of toxic staff relationships, is that positive relationships between teachers matter. They matter because, as Dempsey, Mansfield and MacCallum (2020) demonstrate, they can enhance teacher resilience and assist in negotiating a strong professional identity, which plays an important role in teachers' motivation and commitment. Further, Harris, Caldwell and Longmuir (2013) establish that relational trust between teachers within a school provides a foundation for social structures that engage teachers, support their understanding of their role within the school and strengthen their moral purpose in working towards school improvement.

However, we can't have strong relationships without gratitude. Many researchers report on the prosocial effects of gratitude, especially where it has been shown to contribute to building and maintaining healthy relationships and enhancing social behaviour (Algoe et al., 2008; Bartlett et al., 2012; Emmons & McCullough, 2004; Froh et al., 2010; Grant & Gino, 2010; Tsang, 2006; Wood et al., 2010). Gratitude helps us be more responsive to the needs of others and brings us closer to them (Algoe et al., 2013). It also greatly assists in relationships where there is conflict (Howells, 2012; 2021; Visser, 2009). In the context of education, when teachers focus on gratitude their relationships with others improve (Howells, 2014), with a positive impact on school resilience and school wellbeing (Caleon et al., 2019).

In essence, gratitude by its very nature invites us to change perspective and think not only about ourselves but also about our connectedness with others. The move towards gratitude is inherently a call to give priority to relationships. In a school context, this means that we focus not only on the relationships that are easy, but also take on the challenge of working on those that are difficult.

Prioritise relationships

As teachers, we need to do everything in our power to make all our relationships work better. This is the case now more than ever, as we increasingly find ourselves working in time-poor and task-driven environments. Good relationships and collegiality are needed for us to feel supported in dealing with the many challenges currently facing teachers. As we have discussed, if our relationships have unresolved conflict or carry resentment, it is likely that they will be eating away at us and affecting our wellbeing, as well as those around us. In time-poor environments, it is often easy to avoid attending to our relationships in general, let alone those we find difficult.

One of the most important gratitude strategies for Hayley to engage in was to work on strengthening her relationships. A powerful way for her to begin would be to reflect on relationships that are working and uncover how much they are built on gratitude. Hayley was already reflecting on this while longing for the camaraderie she felt in her casual teaching role in her previous school. Her supervising teacher at this school, Kate, knew that relationships mattered. She demonstrated this by always welcoming and supporting new staff and expressing genuine gratitude to them for what they brought to the school. Even when difficulties with fellow teachers arose, she persevered until there was a more harmonious and collegial relationship. Kate was very busy and had huge responsibilities in the school, however she always made Hayley feel that relationships were at the top of her to-do list. In many little yet profoundly moving ways Kate showed Hayley how much she and her colleagues were valued.

Indeed, the reason Hayley got the position at her current school was because of the wonderful feedback she received from Kate. This feedback was full of gratitude, thanking Hayley for sharing her energy and enthusiasm for innovative teaching practices, and her willingness to learn and work in a highly collaborative manner. By reflecting on her previous school experience, Hayley could see that her relationships had worked, at least in part, because of the gratitude she felt and acted on towards Kate as well as other staff in the school.

As a result of her reflections, Hayley recognised that she needed to find equilibrium in her relationship with Martin, for her own sake and for those around her. While her first instinct had been to avoid Martin at all costs, Hayley recognised that this was not possible given the highly collegial nature of her job as a teacher. However, she could see that she needed to find an alternative way forward to make her job sustainable. In addition, Hayley was feeling resentful towards Martin and inclined to wait for him to make the first move. In order to move the situation on, with great humility and courage, Hayley needed to identify what she had power over and could change within herself to begin addressing the toxic effect of this difficult relationship.

Please note, we are not suggesting here that all relationships in our lives should have the same level of closeness or that we should attempt to feel the same amount of connection, fondness or gratitude for all people equally. What we are pointing out is that whether we like it or not, we are always in relationship with others. Healthy relationships are crucial to healthy staff morale, which in turn has a significant impact on student learning and engagement.

Grow your empathy

When we blame others for our unhappiness it is difficult for us to see things from another perspective. Our resentment becomes so all-consuming that it can trap us in a binary position: we are right and they are wrong, we are good and they are bad. Then it becomes all about the injustice we feel they have caused and our pain, and there is no place to consider theirs.

However, Hayley's choice to give attention to her relationship with Martin made her open to considering things from his perspective. This was helped by a conversation she had with her mentor teacher Steve, who – like many others – had noticed the conflict between her and Martin. He apologised about the situation and his own failure to make it stop, because he recognised that Martin's behaviour was inexcusable. Steve went on to explain that Martin believed he should have more standing in the school given his experience and long-term commitment to the community. Yet, each year because of staff adjustments to accommodate new teachers like Hayley, Martin was knocked back on various requests, such as a particular year level, student cohort, team-teaching scenario or specialist subject.

Steve helped Hayley to see that from Martin's perspective, his difficulties with her, and the cohort of new teachers she represented, were the result of a twenty-year history of disappointment and broken expectations. Seeing things from Martin's perspective did not mean Hayley could or should condone his poor behaviour. She was just better able to understand where it was coming from. Hayley could consider Martin's position with compassion: an important first step in making the relationship matter and moving towards gratitude.

Find an impartial friend

Growing our empathy as a gratitude practice does not work like magic and make all the negative feelings we have towards someone suddenly disappear. Hayley recognised this when she talked about the situation in her regular calls home to friends and family. By now, her friends and family had become used to getting the latest update on Martin and Hayley found herself easily enticed into speaking negatively about him. However, by growing her empathy and her awareness of the importance of making the relationship more harmonious, Hayley became increasingly aware of her loss of integrity in these phone calls.

This was a big step for her. Hayley recognised that she needed to process her pain in less destructive ways. If we are engaging in behaviour such as backbiting, blaming, moaning, cynicism and gossiping, it shows us that we have underlying resentment. A more proactive way forward is to speak directly to the person who has harmed us and to resolve differences in a more amicable way, rather than criticising the person behind their back (Howells, 2021).

For most of us, speaking to another about the pain they have caused us can seem terrifying. In Hayley's situation, she was understandably fearful that Martin would take offense, and she might simply reinforce his prejudices against new teachers and make the situation worse. A more effective and accessible way forward for Hayley was to find an impartial friend – someone outside the context – to help process her pain and find a resolution. For some people this might involve seeking professional help. Hayley decided to call her previous supervisor, Kate. By speaking about her grievances with Kate, Hayley gained clarity about her part in the situation and felt the hold of her bitterness loosen. She also considered Martin's perspective again and recognised that his anger might not have been necessarily directed at her, but at the system that did not give due credit to teachers who had put in years of hard work in country schools. Through Kate's considered questions and attentive listening, Hayley began to articulate the ways she appreciated Martin and his contribution to the school community – things she had not even thought of before because of her resentment.

Practise *reconnaissance*

We build gratitude over time. In keeping with this idea, Hayley needed to approach her relationship with Martin in a step-by-step way, growing her gratitude practice slowly. If we approach gratitude with a desire to get it right straightaway, we set ourselves up to fail. We also need to accept that our first steps are likely to feel awkward.

Hayley's attempts to improve her relationship with Martin and grow empathy can be seen as reconnaissance. As Margaret Visser (2009) explains, in her book, *Thanks: The Rites and Rituals of Gratitude*, reconnaissance is the French word for gratitude. Visser highlights that the origin of reconnaissance is the Old French *reconoistre*, to recognise. We express gratitude by recognising the value or goodness in a person and affirming their worth. Visser observes that across all cultures: 'There is in human beings a powerful longing to be recognised' (2009, p. 389). Visser sees this need for recognition as a 'fundamental struggle for identity, relationship, and belonging' (2009, p. 389). If this need is not met, we don't flourish as human beings and there is a very real threat to our own sense of worthiness (Howells, 2021). As a fundamental human need, it's no wonder we feel shocked and disoriented when we don't receive this recognition of our value through gratitude.

Such recognition can be achieved if we recall the giving and receiving dimensions of gratitude. For Hayley, rather than seeing what Martin was taking away from her, she changed her attitude by thinking about what she had received from him. Her small but significant gratitude practice was to write down all the things she could think of for a few days in a row. Given that this was a complete reversal of her inner attitude, it was no mean feat. Hayley realised that Martin had a lot to offer her professionally. For example, Martin was the staff member most often prepared to speak up in staff meetings if decisions were made that would adversely affect staff members' industrial conditions. Hayley also realised that she was benefiting from Martin's planning processes and the scope and sequences he had developed, which were used across the whole school. The conflict between herself and Martin had prevented her from seeing that these documents had indeed made her life better and saved her a lot of time. She could see herself using these in her teaching practice for many years to come.

As she dug deeper, Hayley recognised that she had received even more from Martin. Through observation, she had picked up ideas from him about setting up a classroom, displaying student work, organising a school fair, running an assembly, talking to frustrated parents, moving students across the school without disturbing other classes and so on. She was even grateful for his relaxed work attire and muddy boots because they gave her licence to rethink her wardrobe and start wearing more comfortable, less formal clothes and shoes.

A powerful way for Hayley to act on these realisations would be to find opportunities to offer reconnaissance to Martin. As Visser (2009) tells us, a very important aspect of reconnaissance is that we can't give this recognition to ourselves – it needs to come from others. This is one of the reasons why it's crucially important that we show our gratitude to others.

Make the first move

In difficult relationships we often feel that we don't have any agency, because we believe the other person should be the one who changes, who apologises, who makes the first move towards reconciliation. Ideally, when we are facing a difficult relationship, both parties would be making efforts to shift their attention to what they are grateful for in the other. However, this is rare because we hold on to our resentment as a way of seeking justice. While we are firmly entrenched in this position, it's very difficult to find gratitude (Howells, 2021). This is why gratitude can't really come to the fore unless we can also practise humility and find courage – two essential pillars of gratitude. It takes one person to make the first move and decide to reconcile the relationship.

Using the aforementioned principle of self-efficacy that for things to change first I must change, Hayley humbly reflected on what she could change herself to improve the situation. She recognised that in small ways, she could address her negative inner attitude towards Martin by looking at something she could be grateful for in this situation and what she could learn from it. One area she knew she needed to work on was dealing with difficult relationships generally and she could be grateful to Martin for giving her the opportunity to develop in this area. Hayley's change in inner attitude by taking greater agency was an important first move.

Take action

In making the first move, Hayley needed to take one or two steps out of her comfort zone and practise gratitude in a way that was authentic to her. As mentioned, we need to choose a gratitude practice that stretches us a little, but not to the point of causing any stress or even more conflict.

Even though she had hardly said anything to Martin in the past two months, other than their brief unavoidable interactions, she was ready to take a big step forward by actually expressing her gratitude through concrete actions. Hayley started with one gratitude practice: greeting Martin when she saw him in the morning. First, she did this when no one was looking and then built up her courage to do it more publicly. She did this for a few weeks, and then Martin started returning the greeting. By greeting others sincerely with a heart of gratitude, we show reconnaissance by affirming the worth of that person (Howells, 2018). Greeting Martin in this way made it easier for Hayley to take up other gratitude practices like smiling at him when she saw him, continuing to refrain from speaking negatively about him to her friends and family and even thanking him for giving one of her students some help. From these small actions, the relationship between Martin and Hayley shifted significantly.

Through her greetings, her gestures of appreciation and her acknowledgement of his contribution, Martin started to warm to Hayley. It's likely this was because he was experiencing reconnaissance from Hayley. As we learned earlier, over his twenty years at the school, Martin had come to believe that he was no longer appreciated and his hard work and commitment had been overlooked. It is possible that Martin experienced even greater validation in this reconnaissance from Hayley because it was offered while he was being undermined by the lack of it.

Hayley slowly grew her practice and her gratitude towards Martin. Very importantly, it was with the intention of giving back to him, not wanting anything in return. Instead, Hayley's focus for practising gratitude was to change herself. It takes a conscious effort on our part to focus on what we are doing, on how we are changing and growing, regardless of what is going on with the other person.

Summary

In this chapter, we explored toxic relationships through Hayley and Martin, teachers with very different backgrounds who found it difficult to work together. Their attempts to avoid or undermine each other fostered an unhealthy school environment. As a way forward Hayley reflected on the good relationships in her life, both currently and in the past, supporting her to recognise the role gratitude can play in prioritising relationships rather than avoiding them, as had been her inclination with Martin. This was enabled by the powerful gratitude practice of reconnaissance – recognising another through gratitude.

Hayley's decision to give attention to her relationship with Martin made her more open to seeing things from his perspective and grew her empathy. Supported by a carefully chosen impartial friend, Hayley could also begin to talk through her grievances and make the first move by committing to work on her inner attitude. Buoyed by this, she began taking note of the things she had received from Martin, without needing to accept or excuse Martin's bad behaviour.

Put it into practice

As we come to the end of this chapter, we again invite you to record your thinking and experiences as you have a go at some of these gratitude practices.

- **Prioritise relationships.** What are some steps you can take to give priority to relationships instead of tasks? Can you put these steps at the top of your to-do list?

   Reflect on a relationship with a fellow teacher that you would describe as harmonious. What are the elements that make it work? How could you bring gratitude more fully into this relationship?

- **Grow your empathy.** Choose a relationship with a fellow teacher that is not as harmonious as you would like it to be. Put yourself in their shoes and reflect on what may be going on for them. If you are finding this difficult, grow your empathy by reflecting on what you have received from this person in the past or something you are grateful for about them.

- **Find an impartial friend.** Identify an occasion where you have engaged in backbiting behaviour about a colleague. Has this gained you anything? What have been the negative effects? Decide that you want to refrain from doing this in the future and identify an impartial friend who could be an empathetic listener. Contact this person, making sure that this is not an opportunity to backbite but a way forward in the conflict. Ask for their feedback on the situation.

- **Practise *reconnaissance*.** Identify one collegial relationship which you think may be in need of reconnaissance. Start by writing down all the things you have received from this colleague and what you value in them. To make this practice more accessible, you may wish to start with the professional gifts you have received from them rather than trying to access those of a more personal nature.

- **Make the first move.** Identify a relationship that you are struggling with at work. Reflect on how this is impacting on your capacity to be grateful or fulfil your role as a teacher. Are you waiting for them to make the first move?

- **Take action.** What is one small gratitude action you can take with a colleague with whom you have a difficult or distant relationship? Could this simply be greeting them in the morning with a smile and a heart of gratitude? Is there something you could genuinely thank them for?

CHAPTER 6

Disgruntled and disengaged parents

It was Term 3 and I had made another appointment with Tynen's mother, Jenny, to discuss his lack of engagement in class. Yet again, Jenny didn't turn up and didn't answer my calls. I was feeling frustrated because I didn't know how to support Tynen, who was often falling asleep at his desk or refusing to get involved in the learning program. In contrast, I was also fielding daily emails from an overbearing parent who seemed to have endless unfounded concerns about his child's progress at school. Was there no middle ground?

Josh, Year 5 teacher

An invitation

Do you work in a school where you feel that parents are overly involved? Are they lining up at the door from day one ready to give you advice about how to do your job? Or perhaps you work in a school where you rarely see parents at all? Are they disengaged in their child's learning despite your attempts to communicate with them?

Broken expectations and poor communication with parents can have a significant impact on our capacity to do our job to the best of our ability. Before reading this chapter, reflect on the various challenges that your relationships with parents might present. Please note, we use the term *parent* in an inclusive sense to mean any adult with a significant caring responsibility for a child or young person, including a parent, carer, grandparent or other relative, a foster or kinship parent or carer, an elder or other adult.

In this chapter we explore how gratitude might support us to deal with the daily challenges that arise from these relationships. Building on the gratitude practices explored in previous chapters, we discover how Josh practised gratitude as he was navigating his relationships with both an overbearing and an absent parent.

Can difficult parents undermine our confidence?

The evidence is clear that parental involvement in a child's education profoundly influences achievement at school (Malone, 2017). As Lara and Saracostti (2019) observe, parental involvement is a key factor in children's academic, cognitive and socioemotional development, with positive interactions between families and schools fostering students' self-esteem, social skills, engagement, school retention, attendance and school attachment. Parental involvement can take many forms including communicating, volunteering, disciplining, teaching at home, participating in decision-making and collaborating with the school community (Malone, 2017). As Barker and Harris (2020) explain, family engagement can also involve supporting student learning and achievement and promoting interactions that nurture positive attitudes towards learning.

As teachers, most of us have been fortunate to have positive experiences of parental involvement at some point in our career. We have likely felt supported by parents who are friendly, realistic about the demands of our job and eager to work with us to make sure their children get the best possible education. However, we also know that unwarranted parental involvement can be problematic, frustrating or undermine our confidence. This might take the form of parents who are excessively involved and have impossibly high expectations of teachers, or perhaps the helicopter parent who hovers over their child ready to fix any problems they might experience at school. The lawnmower parent goes further, mowing down any obstacle that could stand in their child's way, placing immense pressure on teachers to make their child successful regardless of their abilities and talents.

Furthermore, while digital communication has greatly assisted parent–teacher communication, it can also put a lot of undue pressure on teachers. Facilitating engagement online can take plenty of time, particularly when parents expect us to be constantly available to respond to enquiries. Thus, we may find ourselves trying to maintain snazzy online platforms and field never-ending emails and text messages from parents, which takes us away from our core business of teaching and learning. These stressful conditions were amplified considerably by COVID-19 lockdowns as many teachers were required to develop online learning resources that could be used by parents.

Parental involvement can also be problematic when our professional status is undermined by those who treat us with disdain. It's well-known that some parents can be harsh critics of teachers. In fact, a study by Billett et al. (2019) reveals that, out of 560 Australian teachers surveyed, nearly 60 per cent reported experiencing at least one incident of bullying and harassment by parents in the past twelve months including verbal disparagement, yelling and arguing on their child's behalf. The misconception that teachers have short working days, long holidays and other cushy industrial conditions does not help. Nor does the assumption that if you have been to school yourself, you know how schools should operate and are equipped to tell teachers how to do their jobs.

Perhaps an even more significant challenge in parent–teacher relationships is the disengaged parent or a lack of parental involvement. This can arise for various reasons. For example, Malone (2017) recognises that some families who might want to participate in their child's schooling are challenged by potential barriers such as socioeconomic status, a lack of knowledge or education, lack of childcare for younger siblings, full work schedules or transportation issues. Of course, there may be language or cultural barriers as well. Some parents have also had traumatic experiences within education systems and associate school with failure and ridicule, making it difficult for them to talk to teachers or even enter the school grounds.

Of course, the challenges with parental involvement do not fall solely on the shoulders of parents. Some teachers can be reluctant to contact home, aiming to reduce confrontation or avoid the stress of dealing with argumentative parents. In addition, the importance of family–school partnerships may not be widely understood, given that most educators have received no or very little specific training in forming relationships with families for the benefit of supporting children's learning (Barker & Harris, 2020).

Disgruntled and disengaged parents

Josh was frustrated by the endless emails he was receiving from an overly involved parent. The tone of these emails seemed argumentative and patronising and the content suggested that both the student and parent were discussing Josh at home and critiquing his teaching strategies together, fuelling their perception that he was incompetent. While this situation was difficult, Josh was mostly preoccupied with the more urgent concern he had for his student Tynen, who was often tired in class and rarely participated in the learning program. His lunch box was often empty, his shoelaces were not properly done up, his clothes were dirty and he regularly forgot his school jumper, even when it was freezing cold.

At the end of Term 1, Josh organised parent–teacher interviews. Tynen's mother, Jenny, didn't turn up for her appointment and offered no explanation for her absence. In the following days, Josh called her several times and left messages but received no reply. Josh's worry for Tynen escalated. He believed nothing could be resolved unless he was able to communicate with Jenny, but it seemed she couldn't be bothered to make herself available to support her struggling son. The only time Josh saw her was when she hurriedly dropped Tynen off in the morning. As she was often late, Josh was fully immersed in teaching and couldn't stop to initiate a conversation.

Josh couldn't help comparing Tynen with other students in the class, as well as his own children, who were of a similar age at a different school. Josh found himself often judging Jenny. For example, he was disgusted by the strong smell of cigarette smoke on Tynen's clothes. He reluctantly started to regularly organise lunch for Tynen, which was accepted eagerly. However, Josh felt torn – it occurred to him that he might be making the problem worse by letting Jenny get away with not making lunch for Tynen. Every time he gave Tynen food, it exacerbated this feeling.

As the school year progressed, Josh's initial feelings of anger and disappointment started to morph into resentment as he was still unable to communicate with Jenny in any meaningful way by the end of third term. Nothing was changing. In fact, things were getting worse. Josh had initiated a meeting with his principal to seek her advice. However, his principal had already made many attempts to call and visit Jenny herself and was also at a loss about how to proceed. Josh started to wonder obsessively: What are this parent's priorities?

Gratitude. Seriously?

Stuck in his resentment, Josh found himself ruminating about the injustice of Tynen's circumstances and Jenny's behaviour. The bitterness accumulated as he went over it again and again in his mind and sought validation for his anger from his colleagues and anyone else who would listen. Over the course of his career, Josh had come across all kinds of overbearing and disengaged parents but had never been affected to this extent.

Josh's whole moral orientation to the world had been challenged by Jenny's behaviour. He believed that a parent's responsibility was to give priority to their children. Josh felt justified taking a stance against Jenny and how she was treating Tynen. Again, as mentioned in different contexts, Josh felt that if he let go of his resentment towards Jenny, he would be condoning her behaviour.

Despite being aware of the importance of the tripartite relationship between student, parent and teacher to improving educational outcomes, Josh felt his sphere of influence was seriously limited in this case. He blamed Jenny for his resentment and believed that nothing would change until she changed so therefore felt powerless. It was difficult for Josh to see any way forward or to initiate any change in Tynen's circumstances or Jenny's behaviour.

Gratitude might also seem inaccessible to Josh in this situation because of the complexities this family were potentially dealing with, of which he knew he only had a tiny inkling. Intergenerational trauma, abuse and neglect, for example, can make teachers feel powerless to make an impact on students like Tynen. Understandably, there's a sense of fatigue and anger if teachers feel they have to try to sort out the problems of the education system itself.

Why gratitude?

Again a call to gratitude in this situation is not about accepting the status quo in circumstances that are urgently in need of societal and systemic change. This is why dealing with our resentment in proactive ways is an important step towards gratitude.

One of the characteristics of resentment is that we feel we have no choice or agency in influencing change and creating movement. However, if we can turn our attention to gratitude, we recall that we have the power to choose our perspective even when stuck in resentment (Howells, 2021). Again, we draw on Visser (2009) who tells us, 'The word gratitude stands for the process ... by which a person's attitude changes' (p. 174). If Josh could turn his attention to gratitude, it would be an important reminder that he has a choice to change his inner attitude, without an expectation that Jenny should be doing the changing.

If we can allow gratitude to be at the centre of our thinking about parents, this will have a significant impact on whether or not resentment takes hold. This will determine the quality of relationships we have with parents and, in turn, students. As Howells (2021) explores, resentment alienates but gratitude brings warmth, acceptance and understanding to relationships. While resentment undermines and destroys relationships, gratitude builds and sustains them. We can see that gratitude has the potential to strengthen the partnership between parents and teachers and therefore student outcomes.

Refrain from judgement

Josh was full of judgement towards Jenny. Neither he nor his principal could find a way forward. What could be done?

The hint of a breakthrough came from something Tynen did. Even though Tynen was largely switched off during class, Josh noticed that he sparked up when he talked about a rap band he had recently discovered. This gave Josh the idea of teaching students to write rap lyrics. It was the first time Josh had seen Tynen excited about a class task. Tynen gave the first draft of his lyrics to Josh for feedback and Josh was more than surprised that his song was about his mother. Josh was deeply moved as he read the lyrics. Tynen thanked his mother for shielding him and his siblings from their violent dad, for making ends meet without much money, for cuddles in the morning and breakfast in bed. It was an awakening for Josh because it contrasted so starkly with his judgement of Jenny. For the first time, Josh recognised that his disappointment was blocking his capacity to see things from Tynen's perspective. Tynen's lyrics showed that he loved his mother and perhaps did not have any sense of the neglect that Josh criticised Jenny for.

Josh started to see that he had judged Jenny without knowing much about her. This grew Josh's compassion and encouraged a genuine need to better understand her. He began by initiating a quiet conversation with teachers who were currently working with Tynen's siblings or who had done so in previous years. Josh also went to the school counsellor who had worked with the family at different times and again spoke to the principal to see if there was more to learn.

Josh's experience of schooling had been very different to Tynen's, because his parents were actively engaged in his education. He had also grown up in a stable home environment. As he grew his understanding and compassion for Jenny, he could see with more clarity that he had been measuring Jenny against his own values, experiences and expectations.

While Josh was still unable to communicate this realisation to Jenny, he could at least let Tynen know about his appreciation for what Jenny had accomplished in small ways to Tynen. For example, he talked to Tynen about some of the great things he had written in his rap song. When he did this, Josh sensed Tynen's pride. In hindsight Josh realised that his judgement of Jenny had not gone unnoticed by Tynen. This strengthened Josh's resolve to refrain from judgement and take this important step towards gratitude.

Identify resentment

Though Josh had started to refrain from judgement, he still had to further grow his compassion towards Jenny. The best way he could do this would be to explore his resentment and identify it for what it was. When we are in resentment it can feel murky. We might be unable to articulate exactly how we are feeling and often don't like to admit we have any resentment (Howells, 2021). That is why we need to bring our resentment to the foreground and give it a name. In doing so we take it out of hiding, which is where resentment typically resides (Howells, 2021).

As Josh began to identify his resentment, he took a powerful step towards gratitude. He recognised that where he had no power over Jenny's choices or behaviour, he could at least begin to change his own inner attitude and address the corrosive effect his resentment was having on this relationship.

We need to accept that bringing our resentment into the light will be challenging. This can be particularly difficult to navigate for teachers. We tend to expect ourselves to maintain an image of being nice, welcoming, nurturing and positive, tolerant of difference and non-judgemental. When it comes to our resentment, any acknowledgement of this might be accompanied by shame and guilt, and perhaps a sense that we have failed in our role as a teacher to support all students and their families.

To identify resentment, it is also helpful to recognise that one of its most distinguishing features is shock (Howells, 2021). Josh's resentment toward

Jenny came about because he was shocked by her behaviour and his perspective of the world was shaken. Everything about Jenny contrasted with his own upbringing and values.

It is also helpful to identify resentment by distinguishing it from other similar but more 'upfront' and dynamic emotions, such as anger, disappointment, jealousy, frustration or envy. These emotions can usually be transformed into e-motion, as in energy in motion, while resentment gets stuck (Howells, 2021). For example, Josh's irritation with overbearing parents was just that – an irritation. He felt annoyed by it but, at the same time, could handle it, put it into perspective or laugh it off. In Jenny's case though, Josh could not tolerate what he saw as her neglect and therefore his initial anger lodged itself as resentment.

Clarify your expectations

We can further identify our resentment by taking up a gratitude practice where we explore one of its underlying causes: broken expectations (Howells, 2021). When we reflect on our relationships, we recognise that they are built on a string of expectations. This especially applies to the agreements made between parents and teachers. Some of these expectations are agreed upon and communicated clearly. For example, teachers might make some attempts to communicate expectations around students' homework, school uniforms or behaviour management policies. They may even, especially in primary schools, extend this to basic expectations around parents supporting students to get to school on time, fed and well-rested.

However, teachers have a whole host of expectations around parent involvement that are often implicit or unclear. For example, while some teachers welcome offers of parent help in the classroom, others find it burdensome. Some teachers assume that parents will actively participate in a home reading program, while other teachers want children to do it independently. Some teachers want support from parents in terms of discipline, while others prefer to handle it themselves.

We are often too busy to clarify our expectations and, in many instances, may not even be aware of our expectations until we experience the shock we feel when they are broken. This lack of clarity also extends to how more significant conflicts in the teacher–parent relationship might be raised or resolved throughout the year. We often start the school year feeling hopeful and optimistic and rarely outline our expectations around how we might like parents to engage with us when things go wrong.

This gratitude practice, then, involves identifying and clarifying our expectations so we can better understand the ensuing resentment when they are broken. To take another important step away from resentment towards gratitude, we would articulate what our expectations are around parent engagement. Even in the absence of parent engagement with the school itself, as in the case of Jenny, we still have the capacity to manage our own resentment arising from broken expectations. We can do this by reflecting on the initial expectations that led us to be disappointed or angry and on the part we might have played in setting up assumed expectations that were not shared. This can help us to not only further identify our resentment, but also to acknowledge our part in the conflict.

For Josh, who came from a family who highly valued education, one of his implicit expectations was that teachers should be respected. Further, he assumed that parents were aware of the complex demands of teaching and should welcome any attempt to communicate about their child's progress at school. It is not difficult to see how Jenny's behaviour broke Josh's expectations.

How might Josh rectify this? We might well ask if an effective strategy for Josh would be for him to lower his expectations of Jenny and perhaps other parents in the school. However, given what we know about the positive relationship between parent engagement and student outcomes, this would mean lowering our professional standards and settling for less. Instead, the answer lies in communicating our expectations and trying to reach agreement wherever possible. In the same way that identifying our resentment creates movement toward gratitude, clarifying our expectations of parents and identifying where these have been broken can help to bring more clarity to communication and gratitude to the fore.

Communicate your expectations

We can try to clarify our expectations of parents incrementally by creating a welcoming atmosphere in our classrooms and leaving the door open to communication throughout the year. We are reminded here of the importance of reconnaissance and greetings, as discussed in the previous chapter, to help to foster a school environment where parents who might be reluctant to communicate could feel more comfortable doing so. This might mean leaving the door open in a figurative sense, especially for secondary school teachers who may not work out of just one classroom. While one size does not fit all when it comes to parent–teacher communication, there are plenty of tried-and-tested online platforms as well as the usual face-to-face meetings and phone calls. The method we choose to communicate with needs to be agreed upon by both parents and teachers.

As we have seen in the situation with Josh and Jenny, sometimes we need to accept that despite our efforts to communicate with parents, we might not always be able to connect with them so that we can clarify our expectations. Though we can still ask ourselves are there any other ways that I can encourage this parent to communicate with me other than the ones I have already tried? How can I value more fully the spontaneous teacher–parent interaction by being less distracted? For example, am I looking at a screen when parents drop their children off in the morning?

This is also an opportunity for teachers to reflect on and clarify the limits of their ability to engage in parent communication. This would enable them to avoid breaking the expectations of overly demanding parents and any ensuing resentment that might arise. Here, Josh could ask: How can I support overbearing parents so that they feel listened to without giving in to their demands for an unrealistic amount of communication? Again, reconnaissance would be very helpful in this regard to help the parent feel valued, despite our inability to offer them more time or communication.

By reflecting on questions like this, Josh could see that he had not communicated clearly with Jenny, or any other parent for that matter, about his expectations of parents to be active and supportive participants in their children's education. There was plenty of literature, websites and policy documents he could have shared with parents to explain the pedagogical reasons underpinning this expectation, however he had failed to see that there might be parents who did not already share or understand this expectation. By realising that his resentment for Jenny had come from his broken expectations, Josh was able to move from a position of confrontation and judgement to one of conciliation.

Josh was also able to reflect on the fact that he had not been clear about his expectations around unwarranted parental involvement. Josh came to accept that the overbearing parent, who was communicating too much and stepping in to resolve minor, everyday problems for their child, had also broken his expectations. This was because Josh had not been clear about his expectation that students would be encouraged to grow their autonomy and resilience. Again, Josh could have communicated his knowledge and resources on the long-term effects of helicopter parenting with all parents and students to clarify this expectation.

Clarify parents' expectations

> *In order to engage in true dialogue with our students, we educators will first have to engage in true dialogue with their parents. We will need trust and cooperation in a genuine attempt to educate. (Noddings, 1984, p. 184)*

An additional gratitude practice is clarifying parents' expectations of us as teachers and their expectations of schooling more broadly by creating spaces for open and inclusive dialogue (Lucas, 2006). While we need to clarify our own expectations of parents, we also need to be aware that a breakdown in communication and conflict may arise if parents' expectations have been broken.

In Josh's case, it was clear that the overbearing parent had expectations of him as a teacher that were unrealistic. Josh was able to withstand this parent's complaints and respond amiably and professionally because it would be impossible for any teacher to keep this parent happy, and his colleagues had concurred. However, Josh also reflected on the possibility that this parent's expectations might have been broken. Given that the channels of communication were open with this parent, unlike with Jenny, Josh invited him in to talk so that they could both clarify their expectations. Josh was able to do this by explaining his intention to foster student autonomy and resilience. He then invited the parent to share their own expectations and made a genuine attempt to listen and understand their perspective.

Josh discovered that this parent's concern was for their child's psychological safety at school as they had been bullied the previous year. This parent's expectation was that Josh would keep a close eye on this situation but up until now they had not found the words to communicate this clearly. Because Josh had taken the time to listen, he could then respond by reassuring this parent about the strong network of friends the child had in class, his enthusiastic engagement and other signs that he was doing well. As a result of this communication, the emails started to slow down.

Clarifying Jenny's expectations was much more problematic given that the channels of communication with her were not open, despite Josh's attempts. However, Josh was able to reflect on the conversations he had had with staff who had worked with the family. Josh had learned that Jenny had experienced a great deal of trauma, related not only to recent domestic violence incidents but also to her own experiences of school. Jenny had left school early because of long-term bullying and academic struggles, and her parents were not involved in her education at all. This helped him better understand Jenny's disengagement through the lens of her broken expectations, even though he could not talk to her directly about this. He saw that Jenny might find it difficult to know how to engage in a school context that evoked memories of feeling unsafe and not belonging.

Unfortunately, as we have discussed, there can be sociocultural barriers for many parents which make it difficult for them to communicate with the school, let alone share their expectations of schooling with teachers. There is also limited opportunity for parents to communicate their expectations to teachers when they are busy with the competing demands of family life. However, any attempts to initiate this process and create spaces for open and inclusive dialogue are powerful gratitude practices. While some parents may not accept the invitation, the invitation itself demonstrates that we want to understand the expectations of the parents we are working with, to recognise them more fully for who they are rather than who we expect them to be.

Ask the right questions

Our next gratitude practice to help the clarification of expectations involves developing the art of asking the right questions. We might ask parents at the beginning of the year or as the opportunity arises questions like: What are your hopes for your child at school? What is most important to you? What do you want them to get out of school? What are you looking forward to on their behalf? What are you concerned or worried about on their behalf? If we do not ask these questions, we might approach our teaching practice with a misconception that all that matters to parents is improving grades.

No matter what level of education, some teachers might be surprised to learn that many parents do not automatically go to 'good grades' in response to these questions. Parents will often answer by talking about the importance of happiness, fun, a sense of safety and good friendships for their children. The gratitude practice we offer, then, involves asking the right questions to understand the expectations of parents. We need to do this in an ongoing way – not just at the beginning of the year – because parents' expectations might change over time. We can then refer to parents' expectations often, allow them to inform our practice, build them into our educational goals and draw explicit connections between our own expectations and those of parents.

Nurture partnerships with parents

In finding out more about Jenny's background Josh was better able to refrain from judgement and practise gratitude by prioritising his relationship with Jenny. He could see that he needed to value and nurture this relationship as much as he valued his goals around teaching Tynen. As we have learnt in previous chapters, prioritising relationships and nurturing partnerships with parents is an essential gratitude practice. By focusing solely on championing Tynen and improving his learning outcomes in class, Josh had reduced his relationship with Jenny to what philosopher Martin Buber (1958) describes as an 'I–It' relationship, where we treat people as means to our own ends. Josh was only seeing Jenny as a means to achieve goals for Tynen. This is in contrast to Buber's recommendation that we develop an 'I–Thou' relationship. In an 'I–Thou' relationship we connect with another as an end in itself, because they matter and our relationship with them matters (Howells, 2021).

In this vein, Barker and Harris (2020) recommend we embed parent engagement into school life, rather than treat it as an add-on or separate to core business. Barker and Harris suggest that we keep the doors open, foster conversations, celebrate and share positives and identify opportunities to build partnerships with families in creative and ongoing ways. As they point out:

> Parents and families need to know how important their continued support for learning is, and that as the experts in their child they are an extremely valuable resource to be harnessed. Educators have a vital role to play here. (Barker & Harris, 2020, p. 24)

Josh recognised that it was difficult to nurture a partnership with Jenny because he had been unable to meet or communicate with her. However, there were some small steps he could take. For example, Josh realised that his attempts to communicate with Jenny so far had been fraught with worry about Tynen and underpinned by resentment. Not once had he attempted to make contact to celebrate Tynen's achievements, despite knowing that it is best practice to share positives as well as concerns about students with their parents.

Tynen's rap song was an opportunity to celebrate a positive. He photocopied Tynen's work and sent it home with a short note: 'Hi Jenny. I just wanted to share Tynen's thoughtful rap song. It inspired us all!' After this, Josh made a commitment to do something similar once a week: to notice and record Tynen's achievements and share them with Jenny in some way. He did this with a heart of gratitude for the opportunity Jenny had given him to teach Tynen and to grow as a teacher.

This small step also enabled Josh to feel less awkward greeting Jenny and making eye contact when she dropped Tynen off. In the past, Josh had been preoccupied by the fact that she had brought Tynen to school late and interrupted his class. Now, he was able to smile and quickly ask if she had seen the latest sample of work he'd sent her, a question that involved Jenny in a positive way.

Say thank you

Building on this small gesture of gratitude, Josh was eventually able to thank Jenny cheerfully for getting Tynen to school – 'Great to see you Tynen. Thanks for getting him here Jenny!' By refraining from judgement, Josh could now see it was a small miracle she had managed to get him to school at all. Even calling out her name in this lighthearted way felt like a significant step out of resentment and towards gratitude. It also helped Josh to prioritise his relationship with Jenny as an end in itself, which in turn, informed his overall approach to teaching as he more clearly recognised the need to nurture partnerships with parents.

One of the most meaningful ways for teachers to say thank you is to tell parents what we are truly grateful for in teaching their children. Parents, like students, appreciate explicit feedback so we need to try to communicate the precise behaviour we have seen that we are grateful for. For some teachers this will come naturally, for others it takes practice. It's important to find ways that feel authentic and that are right for us and try to build these into our daily interactions with parents. Expressing our gratitude to parents for any small involvement will make a big difference to our capacity to nurture partnerships. As we will explore in the following chapter, we also need to express gratitude in meaningful, respectful and sensitive ways. It helps to be aware that we are more likely to express gratitude in the ways we like to receive it, without recognising that it may be completely inappropriate or miss the mark for others. We therefore need to get to know the other person well enough to be able to express gratitude in ways in which they feel truly recognised to further build those partnerships long-term.

Summary

It is important to finish by underscoring the fact that in our story, Jenny's behaviour did not change in any obvious way. This again highlights an important feature of all of our gratitude practices: when we express gratitude to others, including parents, we need to avoid becoming disappointed when our gratitude is not recognised or reciprocated. Further, we cannot draw the conclusion that our gratitude practices did not work because the other person did not change. When we are truly practising gratitude, we don't expect others to change, nor do we want anything in return. This would be a misinformed notion of gratitude and in itself a seed of broken expectations and resentment.

Instead, our focus should be on identifying the resentment residing in us and seeking to create movement away from this by taking small steps towards gratitude. We can aim to clarify our expectations of others and the expectations they hold of us and notice where these expectations might have been broken, miscommunicated or caused resentment. In addition, we can make efforts to refrain from judging parents too quickly. It would also be helpful to try to understand their perspective, learn more about them and grow our compassion. We can seek to nurture partnerships with parents and prioritise our relationships with them by creating spaces for inclusive and meaningful communication wherever we can.

Put it into practice

You might like to choose one or two of the following gratitude practices that are relevant to your relationships with parents in your current context and record your thinking in your gratitude journal or in discussions with colleagues.

- **Refrain from judgement.** What can you learn about the demographic of the community you work in? For example, what are the employment statistics? What sort of work are parents doing?

What level of schooling have they attained themselves? What were their experiences of school? How does all of this compare or contrast with your own experiences of school, and your parents' values regarding education? How might this influence your judgement of the parents you are working with?

- **Identify resentment.** Reflect on a relationship with a parent you feel is unresolved and for whom you harbour a grudge. Does the word resentment help to explain where you are at? Do you sense an injustice? Have your broken expectations left you feeling shocked and unable to move on?

- **Clarify your expectations.** Do an audit of the expectations you and the school already explicitly communicate with parents. Have a conversation with a trusted colleague about the implicit expectations you have of parents. Are your expectations realistic and reasonable? Reflect on how broken expectations may have led to resentment.

- **Communicate your expectations.** Come up with a plan to create a channel for communication with parents so you can learn more about each other's expectations in an ongoing way. Are the forms of communication you are using already inclusive enough, while still manageable for you? Is anyone missing out, for example, because of literacy levels, access to online resources or being time-poor?

- **Clarify parents' expectations.** How can you create a more welcoming atmosphere in your classrooms and school corridors so that parents feel comfortable communicating their expectations and are able to learn about yours? How might heartfelt greetings help with this?

- **Ask the right questions.** Identify a colleague who has a reputation for having a good relationship with parents. Find out about the kinds of questions they ask parents to clarify expectations. Craft some questions to ascertain parents' hopes and priorities for their children.

- **Nurture partnerships with parents.** How can you invite parents into dialogue with you in a warm, friendly and inclusive way? What small gestures can show that you are ready to listen? Do they feel comfortable addressing you by your preferred name? Do you feel comfortable doing the same with them? Are they aware of the times they can pop in for a quick chat and how to make an appointment for a longer conversation?

- **Say thank you.** Practise thanking parents for the opportunity they give you to teach their child. Think about how you could express your gratitude in a way that is authentic, and in keeping with your teacher identity, perhaps beginning with: 'I'm very lucky to teach your child because …' or 'Thank you for giving me the opportunity to teach your child because …' How might you build your relationship with parents so that you can express your gratitude in ways that are meaningful to them?

CHAPTER 7
Belittled teachers

In the staffroom, my eye was drawn to a newspaper article on technological advancements which was disparaging teachers who were not up-to-date. It touched a raw nerve. I was already feeling belittled by the younger teachers, the 'digital natives', who seemed intent on dismissing me and other older teachers as antiquated luddites ready for the scrap heap.

Margaret, secondary English teacher

I was in my second year out and excited to start at a new school. But only three weeks in and I was feeling humiliated by the belittling comments being made by some older, more experienced teachers about 'reinventing the wheel' and my 'experimental' practices which were apparently doomed to fail.

Oliver, secondary English teacher

An invitation

Have you experienced a colleague dismissing you or deliberately undermining you in front of your students, parents or other staff members? Maybe these feelings of inferiority come from being subjected to teasing, being scoffed at by a fellow staff member or being ignored when you voice your concerns? Have you experienced the condescending nature of ageism, ridiculed as an older teacher for being out-of-touch or as a younger teacher for your lack of experience?

Perhaps your reasons for feeling belittled go beyond your immediate relationships at work. Do you feel that teaching is not only undervalued by much of society but also misunderstood? Are there times when you feel belittled by comments in the media or by policymakers who publicly defame the work of teachers or make unfounded comments about how the problems in society could be solved by better teaching?

In this chapter we explore how we can keep our passion for teaching alive and our resilience strong even when we are being made to feel inferior by various factions. We consider gratitude practices that can support us when we are feeling belittled, focusing specifically on the example of ageism. These include the importance of kindness and building our own self-esteem as well as noticing the power of words to create relationships or destroy them.

What makes teachers feel inferior?

A study by Monash University (Heffernan et al., 2019) of 2444 Australian teachers demonstrated that 71 per cent either disagreed or strongly disagreed with the statement 'I feel that the Australian public appreciates teachers.' This study shows that the majority of participating teachers felt not only underappreciated but also disrespected in the community, public and media. They also reported feeling unsupported and not trusted in their work. Further, when asked if they intended to leave the profession sooner rather than later, 58 per cent of participants indicated that they would, citing underappreciation for the profession as a significant reason.

The media does its fair share of belittling teachers. For example, a systematic review of popular shows on Netflix suggests the portrayal of teachers on screen has had a consistent and significant negative shift during this century (Ewing et al., 2021). The study cites the prevalence of three equally disturbing themes in the characterisation of teachers; incompetence, promiscuity and substance abuse (Ewing et al., 2021). Teachers are also devalued and left questioning their status and worthiness as professionals by disparaging, defamatory, and sometimes misogynistic, comments on social media or online sites that rate teachers, often resulting in publicly shaming them.

The unrealistic expectations placed on teachers by communities and governments during the COVID-19 pandemic might further suggest we are thought of as second-class citizens. While on the one hand, the pandemic launched us into the heroic status of frontline workers, on the other hand, the risks to our health and wellbeing, as well as our families, have been seriously downplayed. For example, there are already ample research findings (Black Dog Institute, n.d.) that show teacher mental health has been adversely affected by unrealistic expectations: to reinvent our entire teaching practice, engage our students in a virtual classroom, combine face-to-face and online teaching, and provide parents with resources to homeschool their children. The fact that this was all expected within such a short time frame, with very little opportunity to upskill, is perhaps evidence of a public perception that teaching is straightforward. There is nothing more belittling to our profession than the suggestion that it can be reduced to a package that can be easily transferred to different platforms of delivery.

Ageism, also known as age discrimination, is another major source of belittling in schools. A World Health Organisation (WHO; 2021) report found that globally one in two people are guilty of ageism. In the school context ageism can diminish teachers and goes in both directions (Buchanan, 2016; Redman & Snape, 2002). Younger teachers are judged by their older and more experienced colleagues as being inexperienced and ill prepared for the profession. They might also be accused of being overly enthusiastic, trying to reinvent the wheel and employing superficial rebranding. Their innovative practices may be belittled by comments like 'that's not how we do it here' or 'that won't work in the real world'. Meanwhile, late career teachers might be accused of being inefficient, comparatively less flexible or relevant, too attached to their familiar ways of teaching and not making the most of the latest technology. They can also be misjudged for old-fashioned or traditional teaching styles and overlooked for promotions in favour of younger staff members.

Belittled teachers

Margaret was shocked to hear Oliver's comment in a staff meeting: 'At least COVID will force the older teachers to catch up with twenty-first century technology.' Margaret had been teaching for twenty years and had seen plenty of young teachers like Oliver come in with their 'modern approaches' to teaching, using every opportunity to make their mark on the school. Margaret knew she was not proficient with technology but had years of quality teaching experience under her belt. She turned to a like-minded colleague, Hazel and rolled her eyes.

Later, Margaret and Hazel debriefed over a coffee in the staffroom. Margaret expressed her resentment and frustration about Oliver and the group of beginning teachers he surrounded himself with. Unfortunately, his comment in the staff meeting had not come as a total surprise. Margaret knew that he often talked brashly in curriculum meetings about what he considered innovations in teaching practice, with new technologies at the core. During these meetings, he was also quick to put his hand up for extra planning and preparation tasks. He then dominated subsequent meetings, sharing the additional work he had done and condescendingly explaining to Margaret how to use his resources, making her feel patronised in front of her colleagues. Margaret believed Oliver deliberately used his adeptness for technology to put her down, with the aim of building his pathway to a leadership position.

The fact that his ideas were welcomed without any critique, and that his demeaning comments were not questioned or silenced, made Margaret's resentment escalate. She was already feeling deflated by disparaging comments in the media about teachers' perceived incompetence and now had to put up with a different kind of judgement from within the profession. For the first time in her long teaching career, Margaret started to second-guess herself and started to worry that she no longer had anything to offer and that her skills were now outdated. Her feelings of inadequacy around new technologies added to this and she quickly lost confidence in her teaching ability. Her resentment towards Oliver and the situation was also eating up any sense of gratitude she had for her job.

Deeply hurt and cynical, Margaret belittled Oliver in return, complaining to Hazel and others that she was old enough to be his mother; how dare he try to tell her what to do? Margaret also scoffed loudly about the fact that Oliver was still living at home and probably had his meals cooked and his laundry done. No wonder he put his hand up for additional duties. What would he know about juggling work and life?

Consumed by her resentment, Margaret was not able to see that one of the main reasons Oliver was behaving this way was that he himself felt belittled and insecure about his relative lack of experience. From his first day at the school, he also felt dismissed and discouraged from sharing any new ideas about teaching and connecting with students. Margaret was unaware that Oliver's overt enthusiasm was his way of dealing with his own feelings of inferiority caused by the snide comments and cynicism he experienced from some of the older teachers. His over-zealousness was his attempt to gain equity and a balance of power or recognition.

Gratitude. Seriously?

Being made to feel inferior is a major cause of resentment (Howells, 2021). In Warren TenHouten's (2018) words: 'Resentment arises when one is placed in an inferior position, and where harmful treatment is undeserved, unfair, insulting, or injurious' (p. 50). One of the most natural expectations we have of others is that they treat us fairly and equitably. The realisation that we are not being treated as equal or that we are judged to be inferior disorientates us – it can shatter how we see ourselves in the world (Howells, 2021). Resentment becomes our way to gain back power and reassert our dignity. Or, as Michael Ure (2014) states, 'The motive of resentment is … restoration of wounded honor or recognition – respect' (p. 603).

Again, it seems that gratitude has no place when we feel resentment is the only natural way to respond. We try to use resentment to gain superiority over those who have made us feel inferior, believing our actions can help us regain power or a sense of justice. As we have explored previously, it can also cause us to lose our integrity – often through backbiting or undermining behaviour and even bullying. When we feel belittled, we have our radar up for those who are likely to hurt us and we put in place a range of protective behaviours to keep those we feel have hurt us – or might do so – at bay (Howells, 2021). While all of this is going on, gratitude is almost impossible to access, and may seem totally irrelevant.

Belittlement often makes teachers feel dispensable. They may feel they have reached a use-by-date set by others – as was the case for Margaret – and are therefore cast aside to make way for more up-to-date 'service providers'. This can be the product of what Vaughan and Estola (2007) call the 'exchange paradigm'. Indeed, our present educational discourse is dominated by words that reflect this, such as *client*, *service* and *stakeholder* (Dale, 2003), which causes teachers to feel objectified and reduced to simply being a service provider. Since gratitude is all about valuing and acknowledging someone's worth as a human being, it is no surprise that teachers may struggle to experience gratitude when they are objectified in this way (Howells, 2012). Again, the natural response would seem to be resentment.

Meanwhile, when teachers like Oliver are belittled for their enthusiasm and innovative teaching practices, they can also feel irrelevant. This comes as a shock to them, especially if their passion for teaching was due to their desire to contribute to society and make a difference. If met with cynicism and discouragement, it is no wonder beginning teachers feel inferior. Their reality is the complete opposite of their expectations and they are likely to feel resentment. Gratitude would be difficult to find.

Why gratitude?

A strong counterbalance to the exchange paradigm is what Vaughan and Estola (2007) call the 'gift paradigm'. In orientating us towards what we receive from another, gratitude can help us see people as people, not as objects or services, and thus lead us to respect people for who they are and not just what they have to offer in terms of the service they provide (Howells, 2012). When people feel respected and less objectified, their self-esteem and sense of self-worth is stronger. They are less susceptible to undermining comments from others and less likely to engage in these themselves. Thus, the reason gratitude is important here is that it brings to the fore the imperative of fostering a sense of what we receive from others.

For example, if both Oliver and Margaret were more able to practise gratitude by recognising what they received from each other, they might be less focused on each other's shortcomings. On the one hand, Oliver might notice the efficient and helpful administrative systems in place that Margaret had established over her years at the school and recognise what these gave to him. On Margaret's part, if she was to recognise more fully what she received from Oliver, in terms of how she could benefit from his advanced knowledge of IT, for example, she might be more inclined to boost him instead of belittling him. Again, a focus on gratitude might allow Oliver to recognise how his words and actions towards Margaret may be damaging the relationship as well as causing others to see Margaret in a less favourable light. On Margaret's part, if she was able to attend to what she received from her other colleagues, rather than being preoccupied with what was being taken away from her by Oliver's belittling behaviour, there would be less likelihood for resentment to fester and linger.

Look in the mirror

By force of circumstances, Margaret was prompted to engage in our first gratitude practice in this chapter – look in the mirror. Her resources for the week needed to be online and available to students by the end of the day. She had prepared, recorded and uploaded the resources, but in reviewing them she realised her audio had been off! There was no way she could do it all again in time. Margaret went to her principal who provided a solution that necessarily involved asking Oliver for help and offering him her help in return.

Oliver was preparing resources for the same year level, so Margaret could ask him to share these with her students too. Oliver might also be able to provide some tips on recording for next time. On her principal's advice, to return the favour, Margaret could look over the resources and offer Oliver some feedback on his lesson planning and assessment of learning outcomes. In providing a solution to this problem, the principal had recognised not only Oliver's expertise and unique offerings as a teacher, but also Margaret's.

Margaret's initial reluctance to approach Oliver because of her underlying resentment was lessened through this reconnaissance she received from her principal. Margaret took a few deep breaths as she walked towards Oliver's classroom. She explained her situation to Oliver and the principal's proposed solution. Oliver willingly showed Margaret how to upload his resources to share with her students and ensure the audio was on in future. They agreed to meet later that day so that Margaret could give Oliver feedback on his resources.

However, when they met she noticed that Oliver seemed fearful of her feedback. Through careful prompting and gentle questioning, she discovered that he had felt intimidated and dwarfed by her extensive experience. For the first time, Margaret was able to step out of her own pain and see, quite clearly, that she was making Oliver feel worse and had even undermined him in front of her colleagues. She could understand more fully Oliver's seeming arrogance and superiority which were making up for the lack of confidence and self-worth that her actions were exacerbating. Although Margaret still could not accept Oliver's tendency to put down older teachers she could now at least understand his motivation.

In reflecting on this interaction, Margaret took a good look in the mirror. Margaret started to realise that while she felt belittled by Oliver, she was in fact belittling him in return. The inner attitude she brought to their meetings meant she was quick to talk over him, dismiss his suggestions, and scoff and roll her eyes when he used the latest educational buzzwords. Margaret's inner attitude helped to create an environment in which Oliver, and perhaps other beginning teachers, were stressed and trying to go above and beyond to demonstrate their competence.

By seeing this situation as an opportunity to look in the mirror, Margaret needed to be honest about the ways she was slandering and undermining Oliver in an attempt to alleviate her own feelings of inferiority. She now realised that doing this only further undermined trust and collegiality throughout the school. Indeed, she was herself participating in ageism by questioning Oliver's ability to do his job well given his age. Margaret could see that she needed to find a way to stop focusing on the pain she was feeling and instead focus on the pain she was causing. In doing this, Margaret could begin to address the distortion and conflict that generated resentment in her relationship with Oliver.

Be conscious of the power of words

The next gratitude practice we are exploring here is to recognise that the words we use have the power to grow resentment or to grow gratitude. Teachers witness this every day when they become conscious of the way their words can sometimes unintentionally undermine their students. It does not take much to do this because of the power that is inherent in the teacher–student relationship. A good teacher notices the way a student puts their head down or looks away when unintentionally made to feel small or inadequate. The teacher can see the light go out in a student's eyes when their contribution is unthinkingly dismissed or when another student's efforts are acknowledged but not theirs. Unfortunately, a teacher's awareness may not always extend to the impact of their words on their colleagues.

The culture of the school also sets the tone for the kinds of words we choose. If this is a toxic environment or if we are working under a lot of stress and adverse conditions, words that arise from resentment are accepted as the norm. As we have explored, when we are resentful we tend to use words that undermine, belittle, bully, backbite or ridicule. On the other hand, the words *thank you* have power and can set a positive tone for the classroom and the whole school (Howells, 2012). When authentic and meaningful, these words make people feel acknowledged for their inherent worth or contribution (Howells, 2012). As Howells (2014) demonstrates, when students are offered greetings with an inner attitude of gratitude, they are more engaged and feel more connected to their teachers, the subject matter and their school. Likewise, as we have explored, seemingly simplistic words of greeting, when underpinned by a heart of gratitude, can have a marked impact on our relationships with our colleagues.

Margaret's shock that her words were undermining Oliver made her realise that she needed to be more conscious of her choices from here on. Along with this was an awareness that although she might not always get it right, at least she could now recognise when she had gone off track. She could attempt to address this with words to boost the other person rather than undermine them. This is the hallmark of a reflective teacher, and one who is practising gratitude.

Distinguish between critique and backbiting

Distinguishing between critique and backbiting is an important gratitude practice because we can be deceived into thinking that backbiting is a sign of intellectual competence (Howells, 2012; 2021). Critique is an objective process of evaluating things and engaging in analytical thinking to make an assessment about ideas. Backbiting, in contrast, is usually fuelled by resentment directed towards another person (Howells, 2021).

After increasing her awareness of the negative impact of her backbiting about Oliver, Margaret was compelled to have an honest conversation with Hazel. Margaret needed to express her shame in making Hazel complicit in fostering resentment towards Oliver. Margaret shared with Hazel her realisation that she had felt justified in criticising Oliver because someone needed to claw back respect from these younger teachers. However, Margaret could now see that this was just backbiting in a different way and that they were both losing integrity with their colleagues and making the younger teachers feel dismissed.

Importantly, by stepping away from resentment and backbiting, Margaret was still able to think critically and express her opinions about best practice and the use of technology in teaching. For example, Margaret did not need to accept that an overreliance on computers and online classrooms was the be all and end all, as Oliver seemed to suggest at times. In fact, using words that incite gratitude could help Margaret think clearly and creatively and express her critique in ways that could at least be better understood by others. Considering the pros and cons of alternative ways of teaching might indeed clarify the reasons why Margaret had chosen to stick to her chosen teaching methods for so long. Her inner attitude of gratitude could give her greater capacity to analyse innovations offered by Oliver and other beginning teachers with an open heart and mind, bringing a renewed sense of wonder, inspiration and appreciation to her teaching endeavours. This is the true nature of effective critique (Howells, 2021).

Be kind

Alongside the research on the role of gratitude to create a positive educational environment, there is also research on the role of kindness (Clegg & Rowland, 2010; Kaplan et al., 2016). Indeed, by its very nature, kindness involves thoughts and actions that are driven by a feeling of compassion and concern about another's welfare. When we think about the sort of words we could use for our students and colleagues to feel more connected and words that build them up rather than make them feel inferior, we would quite likely think of words that are kind. Kindness can be a way of building caring relationships, filling our heart and experiencing gratitude for another person. For Margaret, a powerful gratitude practice she began to adopt was kindness, not only in words but also in other ways such as aiming for more inclusivity and camaraderie, especially with the younger teachers.

Margaret became more aware of just how unkind her words had been, but also how damaged she had felt by the unkindness of Oliver. We are reminded that the intention of gratitude is to change ourselves, not others. This chapter is about what Margaret was doing to grow her gratitude, not what Oliver was doing in return. Margaret started to see that kindness was a measure of her professional ethic.

The act of being kind can also loosen the hold of our resentment. It can bring us into a compassionate way of being that connects us with the other person rather than alienating ourselves from them. The kindest words we can say when we are trying to resolve conflict, are '… because this relationship matters to me', or '… because you matter to me'. This can instantly show the other person that we are making this move because we value our connection with them, rather than having another agenda or serving our own ends (Howells, 2021).

Through her gratitude practice of kindness, Margaret was able to communicate with Oliver directly and in a more respectful way. Another act of kindness was to put herself in his shoes and remember how insecure she was at an early stage of teaching, so she could better understand how he felt. From that point forward, she was able to connect with him on a heart level, showing greater compassion and understanding.

Learn from those who do gratitude well

Prue, another teacher who Margaret worked with, was well-known for her capacity to boost others. Prue managed to offer reconnaissance in ways that were sincere and seemed to come naturally to her. There was a certain reverence in the way she interacted with others, regardless of their status or standing in the school. Margaret would often wonder how she did this. Was it part of her upbringing? Her personality? A trait that some people were born with? One of the most effective ways to become better at offering gratitude in the form of reconnaissance is to find someone who is good at it and try to learn the qualities and skills they model. It is important to acknowledge that we do not need to draw on these abilities from within ourselves, but that we can learn from those who have mastered them (Howells, 2021). It is also important to do this in ways that are natural and authentic to us.

This is what Margaret decided to do: she observed Prue more closely for a week and recalled other instances in the past where she had noticed the ways in which Prue made others feel good about themselves. Margaret then wrote down the qualities Prue displayed. Her list included kindness, gratitude, trustworthiness, generosity, being there for others, readiness to go the extra step, humility, big-heartedness, being non-judgemental, inspiring, patient, empathetic and an excellent listener.

Margaret then decided to focus on two qualities that were missing in her gratitude practice: being non-judgemental and empathetic. Margaret did this by thinking of all the things about Oliver she was grateful for and by trying to put herself in his shoes, reflecting again on how she felt as a new teacher and how important it had been to find her place and make her mark at that stage in her career.

Focus on your own self-esteem

Margaret also noticed that Prue had strong self-esteem. Prue never seemed to feel the need to put others down. This is a cycle – the more we make others feel good about themselves through our acts of kindness and reconnaissance, the more we feel good about ourselves, the more our self-esteem grows. The converse is also true. As mentioned, although it seems we gain back some power by belittling others, it does not actually make us feel better because we are aware that in doing so we are losing our integrity, and thus corroding our self-esteem. This links to the research on the role of gratitude in increasing self-esteem. For example, Lin (2015) demonstrated that higher levels of gratitude are associated with greater self-esteem, which in turn has a greater impact on our wellbeing. Studies have also shown that a strong sense of self-esteem can grow one's sense of personal power and in turn strengthen one's gratitude (Bartlett et al., 2020).

The more Margaret refrained from backbiting and assimilated some of Prue's reconnaissance skills, the better she felt. She could feel her sense of self expanding with these realisations and she felt proud of the person she saw in the mirror. She realised that growing her own self-esteem was not just about refraining from judging herself but also by acting with integrity. It was about doing things differently so that she could embody the qualities she felt good about and admired the most.

Summary

It is difficult not to feel resentful when we are belittled by others. Unfortunately, the teaching profession is rife with external elements that can make us feel diminished. When this is coupled with colleagues who put us down, we can feel even more deflated. Moreover, we can find ourselves in a vicious cycle if we take part in belittling others as this only further diminishes us and our profession. The ongoing quest to develop our character as teachers is greatly enhanced when we humbly ask ourselves if the belittlement we are experiencing from others is actually mirroring back something we are doing ourselves.

Identifying our resentment and its damaging impact is a crucial first step in moving towards gratitude. When we act on what we need to change, we are not only changing ourselves for the better but allowing gratitude to come to the fore more easily, while loosening the hold of resentment. Authentic expressions of gratitude have a particularly powerful capacity to make people feel acknowledged and boosted and can offer an important counterbalance to forces that make us feel inferior. We can also learn much from those in our school community who do reconnaissance well and do our best to take up some of these qualities ourselves.

Put it into practice

We again invite you to record your thinking and experiences as you explore at some of these gratitude practices.

- **Look in the mirror.** Reflect on an experience where you have felt belittled in your workplace in the past. What is the situation mirroring back to you about your own behaviour? What is the pain teaching you about what not to do to others?

- **Be conscious of the power of words.** At the end of your day, reflect on whether you have made someone else feel inferior in some way, unintentionally or otherwise. What were the words you used? What impact did this seem to have on them?

    Heighten your consciousness of the power of words by noticing how others at school talk to each other and the impact these words have on you, other people and the atmosphere around you? How could you more fully bring words of gratitude to your workplace?

- **Distinguish between critique and backbiting.** Reflect on a situation where you have advocated for change or tried to address a seemingly unjust situation, mistakenly thinking that you were offering critique, when in fact you were backbiting. Were you undermining the person rather than their ideas? How could you do this differently?

    Conversely, reflect on a time that you have pursued a deep and purposeful critique of a teaching theory, practice or idea, while holding an innermost attitude of gratitude. How is this different from undermining others in clever or cynical ways?

- **Be kind.** Think of a situation where someone has spoken kindly to you. Remember a time when you have spoken kindly to another. What specific words were used? How did they make you and others feel? If you are ready, take on the challenge of being kinder to someone who may have caused you to feel belittled in the past, and start by considering how this situation could be seen from their perspective.

- **Learn from those who do gratitude well.** Recall the gratitude of someone who always makes others feel valued. How do they do this? What were their actions and words? Write a list of their qualities. How might you learn from this person by adapting some of these yourself, in your own way?

- **Focus on your own self-esteem.** Do you feel worse about yourself when you engage in behaviour that belittles others? Do you feel better about yourself when you engage in behaviour that does the opposite?

CHAPTER 8

Waste

I made an effort to minimise the waste produced by my class, and I was often on the look-out for creative ways to recycle. However, I was being challenged to make an exception for the end of year celebrations. My colleagues were planning class parties with balloons, plastic cups, plates and straws, and individually wrapped gifts which I knew would be loved for a short while before becoming landfill. I felt torn. If I did not take part, or if I voiced my concerns about the environmental impact and suggested alternative ways to celebrate, I would yet again be judged as a killjoy.

Sophia, secondary environmental studies and science teacher

An invitation

Are you sick of seeing all the waste produced in schools? Given the current climate crisis, do you think teachers should be leading the way in modelling more sustainable practices? Does the weight of this responsibility get you down? Maybe you're still unsure how much responsibility you should take on in terms of reducing waste and encouraging your school community to care about the environment? Are your colleagues, parents and students supportive of sustainable teaching practices or do they, perhaps unknowingly, undermine them?

As a teacher our self-efficacy can grow exponentially when a school-wide commitment is made to educational programs that try to raise consciousness of important environmental goals and processes. This is further enhanced when leadership teams support teachers' efforts to reduce waste through systemic change. However, rather than being tempted to wait around until the system changes, in this chapter we suggest that we can empower ourselves through a series of gratitude practices that can help sustain our commitment to preserving the environment, even when it seems like no one else is coming along for the ride.

Here we discover the role of gratitude as Sophia manages her conflictual feelings about waste in schools. She is able to discover that a change in perspective assists her to focus on what is actually taking place rather than only seeing what is not being done. This enables her to move away from alienating others who do not share her views. She grows her resilience by recognising the gifts that she receives from nature, her original motivation to pursue this cause.

Can we ignore waste in schools?

While it is clear that world leaders must be held accountable for their lack of action in addressing the climate crisis, teachers can also play a role in promoting sustainability targets. At the first United Nations (1992) Conference on Environment and Development, education was recognised as an essential element in generating awareness and cultivating understanding on issues prevalent to our Earth. Findings from this conference connected educational development with a sustainable learning environment and the ability to transform pivotal knowledge into conscious action so that our students can become catalysts for future evolution. Reducing waste in schools is an important part of this action because it prompts students, and the broader school community, to better understand the implications of our daily choices in sustainable practice.

As teachers we also need to acknowledge the severe mental health impacts of climate change and environmental degradation on students. As demonstrated in a study by the University of Bath (2022) with 10,000 young people (aged 16–25) across ten countries, the climate crisis is having a serious impact on their mental health. This study found that government inaction on climate change was linked to psychological distress, eco-anxiety and feelings of betrayal. It also showed that 59 per cent of those surveyed were either very or extremely worried about climate change; more than half said they felt afraid, sad, anxious, angry, powerless, helpless or guilty; and 75 per cent believed 'the future is frightening'. The impact of eco-anxiety on current and future generations can't be addressed easily. However, some genuine attempts have been made to develop educational resources and curriculum content to foster students' sense of agency by supporting them to take action, reduce their own footprint and influence others. For example, the Australian Curriculum (Australian Curriculum,

Assessment and Reporting Authority, n.d.) has mandated sustainability as a cross-curriculum priority, leading to the development of comprehensive educational programs such as *24 Carrot Gardens* (n.d.) and *Getting Started with Sustainability in Schools* (Australian Association for Environmental Education, 2016). Similarly, *The Green Schools Alliance* (n.d.) operates across 48 states in the US and 91 countries, including Australia, creating networks of educators who can work together to empower schools to contribute to a climate-resilient future.

Further demonstrating the extent of the problem of waste in schools is the pertinent example of food waste. The World Wildlife Fund (WWF; 2019) highlights the fact that unfortunately, a plate-to-planet connection is not always made in schools. The WWF (2019) found that an estimated 30–40 per cent of food is wasted in the United States, with schools making a significant contribution, serving more than four billion lunches per year. Similarly, a study in Western Australia estimated that three kilograms of avoidable food waste is discarded per student per year (Boulet et al., 2016). This study shows that wasted food translates into wasted water and energy, destruction of wildlife habitat and biodiversity and pointless production of greenhouse gases.

Are you suffocated by waste?

Sophia's motivation to enter the teaching profession had come from her gratitude for the environment and her passion to preserve it. She had studied environmental science before getting her teaching qualification and as such, was keenly aware of climate extremes and the impact of eco-anxiety on young people. Throughout her teaching career, she had seen an unconscionable amount of waste that inevitably went to landfill: pens, pencils, sharpeners, exercise books, laminated posters, photocopied worksheets and stickers … the list went on. As well as this, the canteen served individually wrapped junk food, drinks in plastic bottles and plastic straws. Even the compulsory school uniforms were full of microplastics that would eventually enter the waterways. In her own science lab, Sophia was often stuck with poor quality equipment which had to be trashed and replaced frequently.

Sophia did what she could to reduce her own footprint and model conservation to her students. For example, she aimed for a paperless classroom and largely succeeded. She also repurposed bottles and beakers for use in the lab and made a point of turning off power points and light switches when they were not in use. In addition, she worked with her students to set up a recycling station and a school garden and examined topics such as composting, the lifecycle of landfill, pollution, First Nations land management, and climate change in her classes. In this way, Sophia felt she had some agency and influence. However, looking at the waste across the school, she felt despondent. Sophia had approached the school canteen volunteers and attempted to offer alternatives to single-use plastics. She was met with resistance because these alternatives were more expensive. It would also mean leaving the current supplier who was a member of the local community. Sophia had also approached the school association to advocate for environmentally friendly, locally sourced alternatives to the current school uniforms. However, again, there was no change because the school association did not feel they could ask families to pay a higher price for the uniforms.

Worse still, Sophia had been unsuccessful in influencing the majority of her colleagues. She was the only staff member who queried the overuse of paper and had failed to persuade her colleagues to consistently use the recycling station and compost bins. Recognising that teachers are busy and current systems tend to be followed, whether for convenience or resistance to change, she tried to share clear and simple guidelines and set them up without too much inconvenience. However, with a heavy heart, she still witnessed piles of food scraps and paper going into bins destined for landfill. Sophia's frustrations would often linger and affected her interactions with others. The lack of support from others made her despondent. She felt she was a lone voice, ostracised and exhausted by the battle. How could gratitude possibly help Sophia to stay motivated, hold on to her values and inspire her colleagues, students and school community?

Gratitude. Seriously?

It is understandable for Sophia to be unable to see any place for gratitude in a system where there was so much waste, apathy and ignorance. Where there is environmental injustice, resentment can seem like the most appropriate response. If we are not paying attention to our inner attitude, the gratitude we originally felt towards the environment can be overtaken by resentment towards others who do not share our views. We may be disillusioned because it feels like our efforts are in vain.

Even if Sophia was trying to remember to keep gratitude for the environment in her heart, she found it difficult to maintain her gratitude while surrounded by those who didn't seem to care. By trying to take a stand at significant events like the lead up to Christmas, for example, Sophia stood a strong chance of being judged as a killjoy. Consequently, her sense of being ostracised within her own school community had soured her gratitude.

Why gratitude?

In the book so far, we have discussed gratitude in terms of our human relationships. In this chapter, we still focus on human relationships but expand on this notion to include why we should be grateful in our relationship with the environment. We consider what we receive from the environment, our gratitude for the benefits it gives us and the greater sense of connectedness that arises as we return our thanks through action.

As a study of Japanese students' attitudes towards the environment demonstrates, gratitude for nature can bring about greater motivation to preserve it (Naito et al., 2010). When we are grateful for the environment and approach our physical surroundings and the material world in this way, it grows more gratitude within ourselves and has the potential to impact those around us. In this way, our acts of gratitude grow more gratitude.

We can also see the benefits of practising gratitude for the environment in relation to eco-anxiety. Gratitude leads to emotions such as joy (Emmons & Afshar, 2021), optimism, hope (Kardaş et al., 2019) and resilience (Korb, 2015) – all predictors of psychological wellbeing. Broadly speaking, when we approach life with a sense of gratitude, we increase our positive emotions (Fredrickson, 2004). If we apply this to gratitude for the environment, similar feelings could be generated. We are more able to feel connected to something beyond ourselves and therefore feel less alone, and perhaps less anxious as a result. Thus, we nurture our psychological wellbeing, better equipping us to feel resilient even if, like Sophia, we are faced with inaction and waste.

Indeed, a sense of what we receive and how we need to give back is often the motivation of many who fight to protect our environment. There may well be a certain unrest we feel at a deep, subconscious level if we don't express gratitude for the environment. When we act on this by giving back in some way, this in turn influences our physical state where we may feel calmer and more energised, leading to greater self-reflection and awareness of our actions and the impact these have on our environment.

Do an audit

Sophia felt like she was losing some of her motivation to keep going with her efforts to get others in the school on board and encourage them to take more decisive action to reduce waste. She was afraid of slipping into the apathy she was experiencing around her and that her own mental health would suffer. She was losing heart. Sophia shared her despondency when debriefing with a trusted colleague, Brent. This colleague frustratingly replied 'We're doing what we can.' Brent suggested that Sophia look around the school and turn her attention to what people were already doing rather than complaining about what they weren't doing. Brent pointed out that he himself was trying to deal with food waste by having conversations with his students. He had even recently purchased refillable whiteboard markers.

Brent's request to Sophia prompted her to engage in the first gratitude practice of this chapter, which is to do an audit of all the things that are being done. Sophia made a commitment to Brent to observe and record everything that was already being done at the school to reduce waste. She would also take note of the outcomes of the initiatives she had already put in place, focusing on what had changed rather than what had not. As Sophia walked around the school, she recorded her gratitude for: the energy efficient light bulbs; the school garden; and the on-selling of redundant furniture, computers and second-hand uniforms. Even sustainability as a topic in the school curriculum was worth noting, as well as the growing bank of good quality teaching resources available online in this area.

Sophia's list also included the signs that the compost and recycling bins were being used by at least some staff in the school. She also noted that the unit of work on sustainability that she had developed was well received by some of her students and had being taken up by at least one other staff member. She also remembered that a few parents responded positively to her note sent home about her sustainability initiatives. In addition she observed that some teachers brought their own lunches to school in environmentally friendly packaging; some carpooled or drove eco-friendly cars; others used public transport where possible.

In the case of her students, Sophia paid greater attention to the ways some of them were using more environmentally friendly materials or treating school resources more preciously. She thanked those who were working in the school garden and making efforts to support recycling and waste reduction. Sophia noticed that some students brought their food in lunch boxes without plastic wrapping, initiated clothes swaps, took compost out for their own class and turned lights and power points off habitually.

Sophia's audit helped her to notice the efforts of those around her, even the smallest of gestures. Through this, she was able to begin to shift her attitude of resentment about waste in her school community to one of gratitude for what was being done. As an expression of this gratitude, Sophia was able to publicly thank or acknowledge some teachers and students for initiatives she hadn't been able to see before.

Find your people

Sophia's initial despondency had made her feel alone and cynical. It had made her miss the things her colleagues were already doing to reduce waste. Overlooking their efforts had contributed to Sophia feeling isolated. However, prompted by her conversation with Brent, her newfound gratitude – even for small things others were doing – helped her to see that she had misjudged some staff and students. Thus, in being more appreciative of what staff and students were doing, rather than what they weren't doing, Sophia realised there were more people aligned with her views than she had previously thought. She took heart from her audit and found ways of being more active in expressing gratitude for the efforts her students and colleagues made. In this way, Sophia was making an effort to connect more fully with possible allies in reducing waste, leading her to enact our next gratitude practice – find your people.

Here we are reminded of the crucial part gratitude plays in building a sense of relational wellbeing. In going back to the issue of eco-anxiety that we discussed at the beginning of this chapter, finding your people can help build greater resilience because of the increased sense of interconnectedness that gratitude brings.

Sometimes it might be impossible to find such people in our school community, no matter how much we try. At these times a gratitude practice can be one of thinking of other situations where we have found our people and bringing more awareness to our gratitude for them so that we can more deeply value the support we do receive. Sophia, for example, was actively engaged with people around the world who shared her views. By taking part in campaigns and marches, and fostering social media connections, Sophia had previously been buoyed and energised by this community of like-minded, politically active people. However, she realised that her recent despondency with the school situation had diminished her original gratitude for the connection she had with these people. Sophia's gratitude practice expanded to a renewed sense of appreciation for these connections.

Finding our people and expressing our gratitude for them can give us the perseverance we need to keep our inspiration and passion alive. However, importantly, we need to note that we are not advocating an 'us versus them' culture where we keep those who agree with our views in our inner circle and put those who do not in our outer circle. Everything we have learned about gratitude so far would direct us towards looking for the good, for what we have received from another, regardless of whether or not they support our views.

Avoid binary thinking

Sophia was again pondering her conversation with Brent and his observation that some of her thinking was extreme. She reflected on the possibility that she had unwittingly fallen into the trap of binary thinking. In binary thinking, we say yes or no to inherently complex and contested issues and overlook the middle ground. In the case of waste, binary thinking forces us to take a side and stick to it – that is, you are either for or against it; you reduce it or produce it; you get it wrong or you get it right. Sophia could see that in the past she had been paralysed by this.

We also need to remember the impact binary thinking can have on our relationships. For example, if we are too dogmatic and divisive in our views, we can easily put students off. The result is that they are more likely to switch off when they hear our voice and, in some cases, the behaviour we were hoping to change will become more entrenched. With this in mind, Sophia decided to turn a blind eye to some students purchasing bottled water. It drove Sophia crazy, given they were all fortunate enough to have an abundance of clean, fresh water available to them from a tap. However, she recognised that if she preached about every bit of waste, she would undermine her student relationships – relationships that were crucial to her effectiveness as a teacher and any further work she might do enhancing her environmental goals at school.

Like Sophia, we are constantly weighing up the imperative to educate others about our passions and the imperative of gratitude, which is to connect and build relationships. Sometimes these imperatives align beautifully. However, at other times, they compete and these times require balance and knowing when to put the relationship first. Furthermore, to facilitate gratitude conversations with people who have opposing views to us, we must avoid trying to make these conversations about who is right or wrong. It is admirable to have forums where we can critique ideas, but in this process we need to avoid alienating those who do not share our ideas. As we explored in the previous chapter, we need to ensure we are criticising ideas, not the people who hold them. Our gratitude should help us to appreciate a wide range of views, developing our value for diversity and our capacity for tolerance.

Through binary thinking, we can forget to be empathetic about why others hold views that are different to our own. However, gratitude helps grow our empathy and therefore our capacity to understand their position. For example, in Sophia's context there was a range of reasons why other teachers were not getting involved in sustainability initiatives. Some of these were because of pressures at home, feeling time-poor or exhausted, or simply having so much on their mind that they forgot. In many ways, it is a privilege to have time to devote to causes outside of what some teachers might consider 'the daily grind'.

If we can listen attentively to the ideas of others, this is an act of gratitude because it's a way of trying to find common ground or at least trying to understand and recognise another's perspectives. Gratitude through attentive listening helps us understand and put ourselves in another's shoes; to see that we have something to learn, no matter what someone else is trying to put forward. To initiate the deep social change required to preserve the environment, such actions are vital in order for everyone to feel respected.

Recognise the gifts around us

Moving forward, Sophia still needed to find a way of coping with the unnecessary waste she would undoubtedly observe on a daily basis. To deal with the repeated disappointment and ensuing resentment that would be likely to prevail every time she saw, for example, a plastic bottle on the ground or untouched sandwiches thrown in the bin, Sophia needed a practice to help her maintain her gratitude. Sophia could further awaken the powerful force of gratitude by returning to her connection with nature. When we behold the beauty of nature and the intricate origins of this beauty, we are brought back to the present moment and what we receive.

We can recognise the gifts we receive from nature by engaging in what the indigenous Q'eros people in Peru call 'ayni', which means 'sacred reciprocity'. Lissa Rankin (n.d.) explains, 'They believe that we must give and receive in equal measure, that we cannot take more from nature than we give to nature' (para. 4). If we take this as a guiding principle, sacred reciprocity awakens us to the giving and receiving elements that abound in nature, acknowledging that there is a mutual exchange between us and nature that creates harmony and balance amongst all of life. It reminds us of what we receive from nature and how nature can enable us to meet all the necessities of life including food, water, shelter, light and energy.

Sophia tried to apply this more consciously and purposefully in her observation of both nature and the material world of her current school environment, opening her heart to what she received. While doing this she noticed how this practice helped her physically, mentally and emotionally. If we allow time to immerse ourselves in this observation process, we are reminded of our connectedness, of how everything in nature is supporting us, allowing the very schools we work in to exist, as well as the immense beauty of just a small leaf or the strength of a piece of wood, for instance.

We therefore develop an attitude of awe and wonder. This attitude reminds us that we should not take things for granted and that in everything there is always something new to see and appreciate. In taking up this gratitude practice, Sophia recognised the gifts around her by extending her gratitude to things like the wonder of the composting process and all its wonderful life-giving properties, as well as the recycling depots that enable her to recycle at least some of the school's waste. Sophia also looked around at things she had not taken time to observe closely before. This included gratitude for the lovely wooden door at the entrance to the school, a tree outside the classroom, the grass on the oval.

Taking time to immerse ourselves in nature and recognising the gifts we receive can often be more productive than engaging in rational arguments with our colleagues about why we should or shouldn't preserve the environment. Indeed, Sophia now recognised that she had taken on this battle in her staffroom on too many occasions and the apathetic response just left her feeling resentful and exhausted. In contrast, returning to her heartfelt and deep connection with nature and the gifts she noticed around her revived her energy for the cause of reducing waste, rather than depleting it. By focusing on her gratitude for the environment, Sophia was better able to bring an inner attitude of gratitude to situations where she found herself dealing with obvious apathy or opposition to her environmental cause. We are reminded of the gratitude practice discussed in Chapter 4, a state of preparedness. The point here is to focus on gratitude for the gifts we receive from nature and fill our inner attitude with this awareness before immersing ourselves in the contexts or relationships we find confronting. In doing this, we can foster our resilience and set the tone – both inside and outside ourselves – for what is about to take place.

As Sophia discovered, this state of preparedness gave her the motivation and energy to protect what she was in love with and so was able to continue to model environmentally sustainable practices, even when experiencing opposition.

Connect with past and future generations

We have noted in the Introduction that we do not have the scope in this book to consider cross-cultural expressions of gratitude. However, it would be remiss of us to overlook the important contribution that First Nations cultures around the world have made to awaken us to the important role of gratitude in the preservation and sustainability of nature – as just mentioned in our example of the principle of sacred reciprocity. Our final gratitude practice in this chapter involves drawing from this wisdom. First Nations cultures inspire us to look back at what we have received from nature and how to take this sense of respect for the environment forward into the future. For example:

> *In caring for Country, Indigenous Australians draw on laws, knowledge and customs that have been inherited from ancestors and ancestral beings, to ensure the continued health of lands and seas with which they have a traditional attachment or relationship. (Woodward & McTaggart, 2019, p. 26)*

Similarly, Prober, O'Connor and Walsh (2011) demonstrate that an increasing understanding and appreciation of traditional First Nations knowledge has made a significant contribution to contemporary natural resource management and more resilient ecological outcomes.

For example, efforts have been made to share unique and complex First Nations knowledge systems and seasonal calendars which have been enacted, adapted and sustained over consecutive generations to inform the care of country in local contexts (Woodward & McTaggart, 2019). As Woodward and McTaggart inform us, by carefully observing the connection between healthy country and healthy people, we can nurture the reciprocal relationship that we have with the environment. As these authors encapsulate, 'It is well understood by Indigenous people that if you look after country, country will look after you' (2019, p. 26).

In connecting with past and future generations, we can also appreciate the very wonder of our planet as a constant that spans the dimension of time. In relation to past generations, we could attempt to attend more consciously to the ways the land we walk on (and teach on) has been preserved by our ancestors, and especially First Nations people. In looking forward to future generations, we can look for inspiration in young environmental activists such as Amelia Telford, Greta Thunberg, Anjali Sharma and Daisy Jeffrey or possibly even the activists amongst the students we teach: what are they already doing to reduce waste, despite the weight of eco-anxiety on their shoulders?

Summary

The strategies we outline in this chapter help us to practise gratitude for the environment in proactive, sustainable ways so that we can preserve our passion, rather than becoming embittered or resentful about waste in schools. We have discovered that even if it may seem like no one else is supporting our efforts for sustainability, through a careful audit of what is actually going on in schools, we can notice some progress and be grateful for this. We might find that there are more people who care about reducing waste than we first thought, and our gratitude for these people can build our resilience.

To avoid binary thinking, we can facilitate gratitude conversations with those who have opposing ideas and engage in attentive listening. When we feel despondent about the efforts of others, we can also feel replenished by immersing ourselves in nature and recognising its many gifts. Focusing on gratitude for nature from the perspective of past and future generations helps us to connect with the things we value in a heartfelt way.

We have found in this chapter that gratitude to and for the environment can give us more hope. It can also help us feel more connected, less anxious and more motivated. Gratitude grows more gratitude both within us and around us and gratitude for nature increases this capacity in so many wonderful ways.

Put it into practice

Which of the following practices are relevant to some of the issues relating to waste in your school? We invite you to try some of these out and record both the challenges and opportunities for caring for the environment.

- **Do an audit.** Take a quiet walk around the school and make note of what has already been done to reduce waste by your colleagues and students. Start to compile a list of these things – perhaps in your gratitude journal – and every time you take note of an item, say thank you.

- **Find your people.** Identify someone in your school who is taking action to minimise waste and initiate a conversation where you can thank them. Try to find a way to unite your efforts. If you are not able to find someone at the school, connect with someone else or a group that shares your views.

- **Avoid binary thinking.** Reflect on a situation where you have made your cause more important than a person or felt repelled by ideas that conflict with your own.

    Initiate a conversation where you try to get to know someone better as a person, someone you have judged as being in opposition to your views. Practise attentive listening, for the sake of the relationship rather than furthering your agenda. Try to find some common ground.

- **Recognise the gifts around us.** Before starting your day, take note of something in the environment around you that inspires gratitude within you. It could be the book that you are currently reading! Consider the enjoyment it gives and imagine what your life might be without it. Think about the human, earthly and other ecosystems involved in bringing you this gift.

    Recall moments in your life when you have felt buoyed and nourished by nature. This could be the warmth of the sun on your face, the view from your window, the trees in the playground. Choose to fill your being with an awareness of the gifts nature gives us and bring this awareness to your inner attitude.

◉ **Connect with past and future generations.** Identify and investigate a way in which a past generation has contributed to the preservation of nature. Adopt one or two things that inspire you from their example to look after the environment in your school. Try to identify a young person in your local community who is taking action to promote sustainability and reduce waste. How can you support or promote them?

CHAPTER 9

When the system fails us

After seven years in the profession, I was feeling diminished in so many ways. The professional learning I had to attend was irrelevant, staff meetings were a pointless waste of time, the workload was unfairly distributed, reports were unnecessarily onerous and I already had an intense admin load. Everywhere I turned I felt the education system was letting me down and it didn't serve my students either. I had tried to make some changes but felt an overwhelming sense of hopelessness because the problems were so much bigger than me. I could see no other solution but to hand in my resignation.

Isaac, primary school teacher

An invitation

Does it feel like you're banging your head against a brick wall in an education system that does not work? Do your efforts as a teacher seem meaningless in the larger scheme of things? Do you feel despondent because the very same system that is supposed to be supporting you is getting in the way of you doing your job well, or worse still, undermining you? Do you feel like a silent or ineffective voice in the wilderness where no matter how much you complain about the system it doesn't change?

We are well aware of the weight of the systemic problems surrounding most teachers today. We also recognise that because of the enormity of this issue, you may indeed have jumped to this chapter first, wondering how we might possibly practise gratitude when the systems that we work in seem broken. While we have kept these things in mind while writing this book, and have had first-hand experience of how much they can undermine us as teachers, our aim has been to invite you to practise gratitude as a way of taking control of your teacher efficacy even in the midst of such challenges.

Our approach in this final chapter is to continue to focus on what teachers *can* change by practising gratitude. We explore how Isaac battles with his decision about whether or not to stay in a system that seemed irrevocably broken and in which he feels oppressed and constrained. We find that gratitude supports Isaac to start letting go of his resentment about the things that seem slow or impossible to change. The gratitude practices in this chapter also help Isaac to find ways to increase his sense of agency and keep his hope alive.

Are you working in a dysfunctional system?

Teachers work hard. We often keep going when we feel exhausted. We hang in there for the sake of our students when we could be at home caring for ourselves and our families. We go above and beyond. Yet, despite the enormity of our task, for various reasons we often find ourselves diminished by the system on many fronts. As Dale Spender (2007) points out:

> *Each year teachers are asked to do more: more national testing, more meaningful reporting on students, more social welfare tasks and more new technology courses. And each year teachers are blamed for more school failures, more lapses of discipline, and more of society's ills. Teaching is the most demanding job ever devised yet the teachers' side of the story is rarely heard ... The profession is so badgered and abused, the wonder of it is that there are not more of its members walking out the door.* (para. 11)

Although Spender wrote this over a decade ago, in many instances the situation is getting worse. We find that teachers can be demeaned by a system that casts them as scapegoats for complex issues such as crime, unemployment, family dysfunction, poverty, immorality, innumeracy, illiteracy and much more. Indeed, some media commentators from outside the system, suggest that if we can 'fix' teachers, the rest will follow. This misconception is compounded by an assumption that teachers earn too much for a relatively undemanding job which abounds with intrinsic rewards, short working days and long holidays.

One specific way in which we can feel degraded by the system that we work in, is when we are made to attend compulsory professional development that is disconnected from our real professional needs.

Avidov-Ungar's (2020) study of professional development demonstrated that teachers from all professional life periods were critical of its compulsory and irrelevant nature, with this criticism particularly strong among experienced teachers. Similarly, McGuire (2021) claims that one-size-fits-all professional development for teachers, even if these teachers work in the same school, is largely irrelevant and a waste of time for participants.

Meanwhile, increased accountability measures, overemphasis on data and a test-driven culture can further demoralise teachers. As Beach (2021) aptly suggests, it is a fallacy to think that we can measure what matters most in teaching and learning. For example, we can't easily assess and analyse our students' personal growth and satisfaction, social mobility, happiness, worthiness, vocational skills and so on (Beach, 2021; Lee & Lee, 2020). Yet, an overly simplistic approach to data collection suggests that our success as a teacher is measured by our ability to reduce the number of suspensions or expulsions, increase attendance rates or improve standardised test results in core subjects like mathematics and English. While these are undoubtedly important, an exclusive focus on these numbers misses so much of the substance and meaning in our job.

The paperwork demanded by the system is also on the rise, putting additional pressure on teachers and compromising both our effectiveness and our work–life balance. As McGrath-Champ et al. (2018) confirm, demands on teachers in schools in Australia are growing and becoming potentially debilitating. In particular, they note the extent and magnitude of time-consuming and cumbersome administration, accreditation and accountability requirements, as well as the collection, analysis and reporting of data concerned with compliance. The underlying system, government policies and ongoing change initiatives are hindering the capacity of teachers to focus on matters directly related to teaching and learning. As McGrath-Champ et al. (2018) suggest, teachers urgently require more professional respect, as well as time and support for their teaching.

The despondent teacher

Isaac found himself participating in yet another compulsory professional development session driven by a single-minded pursuit of better data. This time, the focus was on addressing absenteeism. Local politicians and policymakers had determined that high unemployment rates in their district could be addressed simply by improving school attendance.

According to the school's data, Isaac's students were among the worst offenders. The focus of the staff discussion therefore turned to strategies for getting his students to school more often. While Isaac could not disagree with the data, he found the whole conversation demeaning and oversimplified. His knowledge of the complexities behind non-attendance in his class – trauma, poverty, malnourishment, transience, mental health, domestic violence, illness and homelessness – were overlooked, as were the student-specific strategies he was already using. The senior management team offered a number of generic strategies for improving attendance which Isaac was expected to follow up on. Implicit in this whole process was the assumption that Isaac could fix the problem easily if he followed their directions. He felt furious and professionally undermined.

From then on, all teachers at the school were charged with adjusting their attendance records. While they had previously recorded attendance just once a day, they now had to record attendance at the beginning of each lesson. They also had to call home immediately for any students who had missed school for two consecutive days, record the details and outcome of this call in a central database and email a copy to all senior staff. This requirement added to an already extensive workload and left Isaac feeling even more despondent, because it took him away from his focus on teaching. In some cases, the calls home also had a detrimental effect on his relationship with families, as he was making contact for punitive reasons, rather than for celebrating student successes and building relationships.

This focus on collecting data brought back a familiar feeling of dread he had experienced earlier in the year. Along with his colleagues, Isaac had to administer standardised tests for literacy and numeracy. Before the tests, Isaac attempted to open a dialogue with senior staff about the fact that the tests could be confronting and humiliating for a significant number of his students who were struggling academically. Isaac had not been listened to. Senior staff simply reiterated his professional obligation to administer the test for all students in his class. Seething with resentment, Isaac recalled the data shown at a recent professional learning session which showed the low number of students engaging in these standardised tests in previous years. In Isaac's view, senior staff were again driven by improving this data to comply with policy agendas. He felt that little thought was given to the emotional toll it took on his students and the damage it did to his relationship with them. He was put in a position where he had to coerce them into doing the tests, which told them, in black and white, that they were failures.

For Isaac, a further, glaring incompetency in the education system was the severe shortage of teachers, including casual relief teachers. 'Why didn't the government plan for this?' he found himself thinking or complaining to others when he was required to fill yet another gap by teaching extra classes during his scheduled planning time. It was no wonder it was difficult to attract people to the profession, Isaac thought. Who would want to work in a job where you feel belittled, overworked and constrained by a highly dysfunctional system?

Gratitude. Seriously?

It seemed natural for Isaac to feel resentful about working in a system that was not supporting him, let alone his students. As we explored in previous chapters, one of the major causes of resentment is broken expectations. On entering the profession, Isaac's expectations were that he would be enabled to make a meaningful, positive difference for students in a functional and supportive education system. However, what he found was that these expectations were severely broken, time and again. The dysfunctional system was making him feel helpless and belittled and doing a grave disservice to his students, from the individual school level to the broader education, government and policy level. Isaac believed that resentment was the only way to respond to the injustices and inefficiencies impacting on him and his students.

If gratitude is all about looking for the good in both ourselves and others, it's hard to find gratitude when what we are shown is what we are not doing, or how we are not measuring up. When we are feeling belittled or unsupported by the system, our self-gratitude is also very difficult to access.

Similarly, as has been stated many times in this book, to respond with gratitude would seem to Isaac that he was condoning a system that was failing him and his students on a day-to-day basis. Gratitude can also seem out of reach when we are contemplating how we can possibly enact it in a seemingly amorphous and impersonal education system. It is easier for us to feel like a victim in these circumstances, overtaken by forces or phenomena which are out of our control.

Why gratitude?

When we feel disempowered it is helpful, although sometimes difficult, to try to reflect on what we can learn from our resentment. Often our resentment is nudging us to do something about a situation which we see as unjust or inequitable. In many ways, this is its purpose. However, as resentment lingers, it can do the opposite, where we become so embittered, cynical or despondent that we feel like giving up on our desire to work for change.

Gratitude for what does work in the system could help Isaac shift from resentment to a more balanced perspective from which to enact change. It could instil a sense of hope and optimism, which in turn would have a positive impact on his declining wellbeing (Bazargan-Hejazi et al., 2021) and provide greater life satisfaction (Gungor et al., 2021).

As we have explored, gratitude has the power to create a greater sense of agency because it reminds us we can choose our inner attitude (Howells, 2021). Even though it is understandable that Isaac felt his agency was being taken away, if he were to expand his thinking to consider what he was grateful for, he could begin to shift the focus away from external forces to his inner attitude – something he can control. Acknowledging that you feel resentment and that you have the power to choose otherwise is one of the most important things you can do to take action.

Gratitude for self would further increase Isaac's sense of agency. At times when we feel we cannot be grateful to those around us, and in this case to systems that we feel undermine us, we can bring our attention back to what we are grateful for about ourselves. In Isaac's case, he could be grateful to himself for his years of resilience working in such a system and for his courage and humility in the process. Isaac's self-gratitude would show him that he had been doing his best, given the circumstances he was working in. This is important because, even though Isaac might blame the system, underneath he might also feel a sense of failure because he has not been able to enact more change or feels if he was stronger he would be able to 'beat' the system.

Self-gratitude is also important because it could provide Isaac with a yardstick to measure how much he wanted to keep working in a system that didn't seem to serve him or seemed to go against his values. Our self-gratitude can highlight the limitations and constraints imposed on us by the institutions and systems we work in and help us recognise when these pressures mean we are unable to maintain our overall wellbeing. Indeed, leaving the profession could be an act of self-gratitude because it might be preserving Isaac's self-esteem, reducing his stress levels, or enabling him to make a statement about how he should be treated. Self-gratitude can lead to clear, self-defining actions.

Refine your why

Indeed, Isaac had reached breaking point. His letter of resignation had been with his principal, Angela, for a week when he got a call to meet with her. Angela started the conversation by thanking him for his honesty and letting him know that she respected his decision. She then compassionately asked Isaac to elaborate on his reasons for resigning. He nervously shared how he had felt broken by the system. He shared his frustrations about the compulsory and irrelevant professional learning, the overemphasis on simplistic data gathering, the ever-increasing administrative tasks which took his focus off teaching and the sadness he felt for his students when the education system failed them.

Angela sat and listened attentively and compassionately. She then asked him: 'Why did you get into teaching in the first place? Can you tell me about your journey into the profession?' With this questioning, Angela was prompting Isaac to rediscover and rearticulate the reasons he once had for becoming a teacher. When we are caught up in an amorphous system that seems to have no boundaries, yet seems to constrain us with every turn we take, we can lose sight of our original motivation to become part of this system. Hence our first gratitude practice is to discover, or rediscover, our reasons for teaching and see if they have grown and developed; in other words, to refine our why.

In exploring Angela's questions, Isaac found himself reflecting on the fact that he had given up his high-paying career in marketing because he had a yearning to do something more meaningful. He had watched his nieces and nephews grow up and was energised by their curious minds and enthusiasm for learning. Given the contrast between his own academic failures at school and his later successes in business and marketing, he had also been motivated to give his students an opportunity to experience success regardless of formal grades. Over his teaching career, he had developed a stronger orientation to social justice and recognised that this was his new, emerging why. In fact, this emerging why was the reason he had become so despondent, as he began to see more and more ways the system seemed to let down his students and fail to promote social justice.

Not all of us have the same reasons for entering the profession. We know plenty of teachers who have fallen into the profession because they were not sure what else to do, or because they were accepted into the pre-service teacher course at university, only to discover their why much later.

We also know teachers who went into the profession because they followed the footsteps of their parents. Some teachers are motivated to get into teaching with a view to changing the system for highly personal reasons such as having siblings with a disability who were treated unfairly or their own experiences of being let down by their school. Perhaps a musician who struggles to make ends meet decides that teaching music could be a financially viable career, as well as a vehicle for sharing their love of music. Meanwhile, a highly qualified engineer takes up teaching to inspire more girls into her first profession. Others might end up teaching because they are grateful for the opportunities education afforded them and are keen to pay it forward.

Regardless of our why, rediscovering our reasons for teaching can help to remind us that the very existence of the system we are working in allows us to pursue our teaching aspirations and educational goals. Thus we can begin to consider, with a heart of gratitude, the enabling characteristics of the system, faulty though it may be.

Over the following weeks and months of striving to rediscover his why, Isaac began to recognise that at least some of the components of the education system provided conditions in which he could pursue his social justice orientation. Compared with his experience in marketing, which had focused aggressively on competition and money, the education system still had small pockets in which he could build positive, authentic relationships with students and their families. He was able to find gratitude for the opportunity to work in an area where he could bring his strong passion for equity to life, at least to some extent.

Furthermore, even though Isaac had felt beaten down by the system lately, he was gradually able to see that this process of refining his reasons for teaching helped to strengthen his internal motivation to change the system. By engaging in this gratitude practice and articulating his why, Isaac started to feel like his fortitude and resolve to change things was being reignited.

Speak your truth

Through Isaac's conversation with Angela, he also started to begin to enact an additional gratitude practice – speaking your truth (Howells, 2021). Although Isaac had shared his grievances with colleagues and in some staff meetings, up until now he had been afraid of going directly to the principal. When he did speak up, he did so in a spirit of resentment, often complaining about the system and backbiting the senior management team, but in doing so he was being truthful. However, he came to realise that some of his broken expectations that were fuelling his resentment arose from a misunderstanding. He had assumed that Angela was already aware of his grievances. Isaac was very surprised to learn that Angela seemed to have little awareness that he was finding it so tough. She told him that because she believed that he was such a competent teacher, and he hadn't complained directly to her before now, that he was travelling well.

In actual fact, for most of us, speaking directly to another about our grievances with them can be one of the most challenging things we ever do (Howells, 2021). We might be afraid they will misunderstand our intentions, or make the situation worse, or make us feel wrong. Indeed, Isaac was predicting all these things as he was nervously waiting outside the principal's office. From his perspective, confronting authority was seen as unnecessarily rocking the boat.

However, because of Angela's compassionate approach in genuinely inviting him to share his side of the story, Isaac was able to talk freely and honestly. She even agreed with many of his claims and provided her own experience of similar constraints, especially in relation to the increasing administrative requirements of her job, which put extra pressure on principals. This openness helped Isaac trust Angela enough to be able speak his mind and let her know what was wrong with the system. Perhaps she could do something about it? In this process of speaking his truth, Isaac made a positive step forward, both for himself and others who were suffering.

In fact, Isaac had initiated a grateful conversation. He was enacting self-gratitude by taking a stand and being proactive about things he could no longer tolerate. He was also speaking directly to Angela as the person who might be able to make change, albeit within the constraints of the system that they themselves were working in, rather than complaining about her behind her back – a very powerful step away from resentment towards gratitude. In turn, Angela was expressing gratitude through her empathy and through her encouragement of Isaac to speak truthfully, even though it might have been hard for her to hear and she may not have been able to provide solutions to his grievances.

Speaking our truth is also an important aspect of self-gratitude because it helps us set strong boundaries around how we want things to change.

When we voice where we stand, we become more self-defining and grow our resilience. As an act of self-gratitude, this practice can help us find a way to walk through our fears so we do not let them dominate our decision-making (Howells, 2021).

Celebrate success

Another important strategy is to express gratitude for aspects of the education system that enable us to pursue our professional goals. In their conversation about Isaac's pending resignation, Angela invited him to send her an email in the next few days outlining what he felt were his successes during his time at the school. In writing this email, Isaac reflected on the relationships he had built with his students and their families over the years. He also recognised that while his attendance data was low on average compared to the rest of the school, for his cohort it had improved significantly. He remembered the referrals he had made to social workers and psychologists to get support for students with mental health and welfare issues. He recalled the community contributions he had helped his students make such as public murals, litter collections, tree planting, recycling and so on. He thought of some smaller things as well – like Jake, a student who had come to him at the beginning of the year non-verbal, but had recently started to greet Isaac in the morning, make eye contact and occasionally smile.

Thinking about his own successes made Isaac reflect on the fact that he couldn't have made these gains without the systems established broadly across the school. For example, he started to feel more grateful for the improved transition process for students from primary to high school and the school-wide positive behaviour support and anti-bullying programs. He also noted the improvements to the school's infrastructure in the time he had been there, including improved access for students with disabilities, a resurfaced basketball court and a school garden. Isaac could see how all these systemic improvements had led, in some way, to increased student engagement.

As Isaac reflected on his achievements to date, as well as identifying some of the achievements of the education system he was working in, he couldn't help but start to envisage possibilities for the future. In enacting this gratitude practice and celebrating success, Isaac started to see what the system had enabled him to do in the past, as well as what it might enable him to do in the future. This gratitude practice gave him hope.

Understand your nemesis

It is helpful to remember that a system is a system, not a person. By better understanding our nemesis, we can become clearer about what, rather than who, might be making us feel hopeless or despondent. This gratitude practice therefore challenges teachers to get to know their nemesis by committing time to exploring the machinations of the system they work in. In doing this, we can also become more aware of any possibilities that currently reside within this system that we can better use to pursue our educational goals. As an example, we can often find ourselves feeling angry and frustrated by our most immediate line managers and it is easy to set them up as the enemy. However, by taking some time to find out more about their role and the possibilities and constraints that the system creates for them, we might begin to grow our compassion for them. Furthermore, if we then explore the work of their line managers and so on, we might also start to recognise that what we are angry and frustrated with is not any one person or group of people.

Add to this the significant and pervasive impact of the media and political campaigns around education policy decisions. In these multiple and complex layers of influence, we can clearly recognise that the system governing our work is shaped by many interrelated factors that cannot be attributed to any one person.

As a gratitude practice, seeking to understand our nemesis also helps us to see that systems are not designed to prioritise relationships. This can be a hard realisation but it can also feel liberating when we stop expecting the system to show compassion, care or empathy.

For Isaac, finding his nemesis involved depersonalising the system. He recognised that this did not mean that he should stop caring and advocating for change. It just meant that he could become more pragmatic and not fuelled by resentment, focused on seeing the system as a system rather than looking for any particular person to blame. He also had more energy for nurturing the relationships he did have influence over within the system.

Play the long game

An additional gratitude practice is to acknowledge that we are playing the long game. Systems are invariably slow to change and we need to set realistic expectations for ourselves and the role we can play in having an impact on this change. By playing the long game, we remind ourselves to keep our grander aspirations and educational ideals in perspective, while nurturing and maintaining the relationships within our immediate sphere of influence – those that are in front of us every day, with students, colleagues and families.

Isaac came to an understanding of the long game when he reflected on his colleague, Harry. Harry had started teaching at the school at the same time as Isaac. Isaac held him in high regard not only as a friend but also as a teacher, observing how much Harry cared about his students and their learning, and how he always strived to improve his practice. However, Harry did not experience the same despondency Isaac did and had never indicated he would consider leaving the profession. Isaac would often share his frustrations with Harry over a beer. Harry was a good listener, understanding and sympathetic, but he seemed consistently unaffected by what Isaac felt so strongly about in relation to what he saw as a broken education system.

Isaac decided to talk to Harry about this issue directly, asking him how he remained so positive and optimistic. Harry then explained that his journey into the profession was different. When he decided to become a teacher, he had no expectations that the system would be perfect. In fact, he went into the profession knowing, from his own experience as a parent of school-aged children, that the system was broken in many ways. Harry was a lot more realistic about what he was getting himself into; he had a better understanding of his nemesis before he had even started.

Isaac was gradually able to see that Harry accepted the imperfections of the system and did not devote his time and energy wishing it was otherwise. Harry was quick to point out the things he had seen change and improve over time, which Isaac had missed because he was wanting things to change quickly and more dramatically. He told Isaac he accepted that things change slowly in systems as big as schools and education overall. He had joined the profession recognising this was a long game in which patience was a virtue.

There is much in educational reform that attempts to offer a quick fix. However, most of the time, system or institutional change is somewhat cumbersome. If we are in situations where change on the outside is inevitably slow, the wisdom of gratitude would have us accepting this and put the focus on our own response and our own character, through learning about ourselves in the process of developing patience.

Make a firm decision

With his resignation still on the principal's desk, Isaac needed to make a decision whether to stay or leave. A careful and considered reflection on what we are grateful for in our teaching role can often provide answers and clarity about which decision to make.

If we can no longer see anything to be grateful for and are still disillusioned and resentful after trying, and this situation continues for a long time, then perhaps the best decision is to leave. We might well thrive and find our calling in another profession. There is nothing wrong with this.

Alternatively, we may recognise that we need to stay in the profession because we have bills to pay, or are afraid of possible unemployment, or we just don't know what else to do. However, staying in the profession for these reasons alone may not align with our why, and our decision might not be strong enough to stay the course when things are difficult.

Ideally, if we do decide to stay, the gratitude practices we offer here can sustain us in this decision and guide us in the everyday challenges of the education system in which we work. Indeed, this is what helped Isaac to withdraw his resignation letter and make the firm decision to stay.

Summary

If we have entered the education system with a strong sense of justice and equity, or with high ideals about how the system should work, it is hard not to become despondent or resentful when we experience barriers that impact our capacity to be effective teachers. If we advocate for change and our pleas are not heard or are disregarded, we can very well lose sight of our original motivation for becoming a teacher.

In this chapter we have explored how a focus on gratitude for what is working within the system can help us gain a more balanced perspective and be more effective in how we advocate for change. We have presented strategies that can help remove the blame from certain individuals and to see that they themselves are also working within the constraints of the system. In depersonalising our blame we can reduce our resentment and hopefully be more realistic about what we can expect from systems, while also speaking up about our grievances in respectful and empowering ways. At the same time, we have seen that if we choose to leave a system that is not working for us, this is not failure but a way of recovering our professional integrity and self-gratitude. Hopefully though, these gratitude practices may offer other options, so we can gain greater agency even when the systems around us seem broken.

Put it into practice

Our job is difficult. Hopefully by taking up one or two of the following gratitude practices, you will feel better able to navigate the complex challenges you face when you feel the system is not supporting you. Sharing these practices with a trusted colleague or recording your thinking in your gratitude journal, might help strengthen your resolve and give you added resilience.

- **Refine your why.** Take some time to think about these questions: Why did you go into teaching? Has this changed, and if so, what is your emerging why? On a good day, what is it that gets you out of bed in the morning excited to teach? What gives you hope?
- **Speak your truth.** Identify your fears about speaking up about things that you believe need to change by writing them down in your gratitude journal or discussing them with a trusted colleague. Which of these fears are helpful in protecting you? Which fears are holding you back from speaking your truth?
- **Celebrate success.** Can you find ways in which the education system you are working in has made it easier for you to pursue your professional goals? How is the education system you work in better than the education system of the past? In what ways has it improved since you were a student?
- **Understand your nemesis.** Reflect on the education system you work in. Have you been blaming a particular person for the faults you have identified when they themselves are constrained by the same system?
- **Play the long game.** Without self-judgment, reflect on how realistic you are about the time it takes for systemic change to occur. Build your optimism by taking note of the things that have changed over time and recognising the time it might take for other changes to occur.
- **Make a firm decision.** As you reflect on what you can be grateful for, is your commitment to your job as strong now as it was when you first began? Are you making a clear and firm decision to stay, even in the face of systemic difficulties? Why? Discuss these questions with a trusted colleague who knows you well.

Conclusion

When we thank one of our students with a heart of gratitude, we often get a joyful response in their smile. When we take the time to greet parents gratefully, this too can build a sense of connection and community in our classroom and school. When we approach a colleague, not for something we can get from them but with the aim of giving thanks to them, we are bringing about a deep sense of recognition that can only happen through gratitude.

As you can see, practising gratitude does not require a grand gesture or a massive personality change. It does not require you to feel grateful all the time, nor do you need to feel positive or wait until the conditions are just right. It's a step-by-step process where just one action can create movement in the right direction. Not only is there a ripple effect for those around us but also, perhaps more importantly, it changes us for the better.

Please don't feel that your gratitude practices are not worthwhile if they are not recognised or reciprocated in any obvious way. Ideally, the motivation for practising gratitude in the first place, is to look for outcomes in ourselves, with no expectation of anything in return from our environment or those around us. We can ask ourselves questions such as: Is my gratitude helping me feel more empowered? Am I calmer, more connected, more motivated or resilient? Do I bring greater passion and integrity to what I do? Do I feel more optimistic, joyful and hopeful? Is there an increase in my self-esteem or sense of abundance?

We should not expect to get gratitude 'right' every time we try to practise it. Instead, we lean into the imperfection of gratitude and accept that this is why we call it a practice. When we are bravely bringing gratitude in a challenging situation, it is natural to feel like a beginner and we may feel awkward or anxious about the possibility of making a mistake. However, we can be assured that any gratitude practice we choose to take up, no matter how small it may seem, is significant.

The institutional constraints and everyday challenges that teachers experience can often make deep gratitude seem inaccessible. As teachers, we are not only trying to teach, but are often doing so while feeling time-poor and exhausted, and facing the challenges of angry students, toxic staff relationships or difficult parents. As a backdrop to all of this, we might also feel belittled as a profession and let down by a system that seems broken. It is because of this difficult environment that resentment is more likely to take hold than gratitude. Resentment is the very opposite of gratitude and leaves us feeling stuck and powerless. We hope through reading this book you have discovered that deep gratitude has a beautiful illuminating power. It helps us to see where it has been missing and where resentment resides.

In this book, we do not offer deep gratitude as a panacea to solve all the problems in education, which we acknowledge are significant and ever-present. Nor do we suggest that gratitude is a quick fix, because as a practice we need to allow it to unfold over time. What we do propose is that gratitude gives us a choice in how we respond to the daily adversities we face as teachers.

In making this choice, deep gratitude helps us develop a balanced perspective so we can be more effective in advocating for change. Through gratitude we aim to keep it real, feel empowered to speak up about our grievances in respectful ways and change the things that we *can* change. Through gratitude we gain greater agency as we grow our empathy, compassion and capacity to prioritise relationships, which are at the very heart of teaching. The most empowering choice we can make is choosing deep gratitude and enacting it at the level of our inner attitude.

It often takes time to feel the accumulated effects of gratitude. You may find yourself returning to this book regularly to guide you as you try to embody deep gratitude practices more fully. You might also like to regularly return to your gratitude journal, if you have chosen this as a means to reflect and record your thinking.

Another consolidating strategy is to get together with other colleagues to support and encourage each other in your gratitude practice. As we have mentioned, we have found that book clubs are a very effective way to structure these gatherings and to offer different perspectives about dilemmas you may be struggling with when attempting to practise gratitude. Meeting to share the challenges and celebrate successes can offer strength and motivation for you and your peers. It helps to create spaces for inclusive and meaningful dialogue and navigate the difficult moments of teaching together. Indeed, there is something about the topic of gratitude that gives us permission to discuss and reflect on areas of our lives that have deep meaning, areas rarely shared in staff meetings. We always have an inner attitude of some kind and are carrying this with us from the moment we wake up. This book therefore dismisses the artificial division between our private and public lives as teachers. Instead, it highlights the powerful impact of preparing our inner attitude with gratitude before we start our day or before we enter our classroom. It recognises that deep gratitude reaches into our hearts and to a higher part of ourselves.

Through the voices of teachers who are bravely navigating everyday challenges, we hope that the stories and gratitude practices we have shared in this book help you to feel more empowered and optimistic about the role of deep gratitude in creating harmony both within yourself and your workplace. Our intention has been to show that when gratitude is practised in a consistent and purposeful way, it can help you to juggle the complex and competing demands of education.

Finally, we hope our book has given your own gratitude more life and meaning and demonstrated its immediate relevance to your workplace. Our motivation for writing it has been to share accessible and sustainable gratitude practices to give you a sense of empowerment even when you feel overwhelmed by the everyday challenges that teachers face. Indeed, deep gratitude has its greatest power when we practise it in the midst of adversity.

References

24 Carrot Gardens. (n.d.). *About*. https://www.24carrot.mona.net.au/about

Algoe, S. B, Haidt, J., & Gable, S. L. (2008). Beyond Reciprocity: Gratitude and Relationships in Everyday Life. *Emotion, 8*(3), 425–429. https://doi.org/10.1037/1528-3542.8.3.425

Algoe, S. B., Fredrickson, B. L., & Gable, S. L. (2013). The Social Functions of the Emotion of Gratitude via Expression. *Emotion, 13*(4), 605–609. https://doi.org/10.1037/a0032701

Allen, S. (2018). *The Science of Gratitude*. Greater Good Science Center. https://ggsc.berkeley.edu/images/uploads/GGSC-JTF_White_Paper-Gratitude-FINAL.pdf

Australian Association for Environmental Education. (2016). *Getting Started with Sustainability in Schools: It's Time to Get Started with Sustainability*. https://sustainabilityinschools.edu.au/

Australian Childhood Foundation. (n.d.). *Resources*. https://professionals.childhood.org.au/resources/

Australian Curriculum, Assessment and Reporting Authority (ACARA). (n.d.). *Foundation–10 curriculum (Version 8.4)*. https://www.australiancurriculum.edu.au/f-10-curriculum/

Avidov-Ungar, O. (2020). The Professional Learning Expectations of Teachers in Different Professional Development Periods. *Professional Development in Education*. https://doi.org/10.1080/19415257.2020.1763435

Barker, B., & Harris, D. (2020). *Parent and Family Engagement: An Implementation Guide for School Communities*. Australian Research Alliance for Children and Youth. https://www.aracy.org.au/documents/item/647

Bartlett, M. Y., Valdesolo, P., & Arpin, S. N. (2020). The Paradox of Power: The Relationship between Self-Esteem and Gratitude. *The Journal of Social Psychology, 160*(1), 27–38. https://doi.org/10.1080/00224545.2019.1601609

Bartlett, M. Y., Condon, P., Cruz, J., Baumann, J., & Desteno, D. (2012). Gratitude: Prompting Behaviours that Build Relationships. *Cognition and Emotion*, 26(1), 2–13. https://doi.org/10.1080/02699931.2011.561297

Baumeister, R. F., Bratslavsky, E., Finkenaur, C., & Vohs, K. D. (2001). Bad is Stronger than Good. *Review of General Psychology, 5*(4), 323–370. https://doi.org/10.1037/1089-2680.5.

Bazargan-Hejazi, S., Dehghan, K., Chou, S., Bailey, S., Baron, K., Assari, S., Marzio, R., Teklehaimanot, S., Kermah, D., Lindstrom, R. W., Shirazi, A., Lopez, D., Bazargan, M. (2021). Hope, Optimism, Gratitude, and Wellbeing among Health Professional Minority College Students. *Journal of American College Health*, 1–9. https://doi.org/10.1080/07448481.2021.1922415

Beach, J. M. (2021). *Can We Measure What Matters Most?: Why Educational Accountability Metrics Lower Student Learning and Demoralize Teachers*. Rowman & Littlefield.

Bernstein, C., & Batchelor, T. P. (2022). Qualitative Exploration of Workplace Demands, Resources and Bullying among Teachers in South African Schools: Implications for Individual and Organisational Well-being. *South African Journal of Education, 42*(2), 1–9. https://dx.doi.org/10.15700/saje.v42n2a2081

Bernotaite, L., & Malinauskiene, V. (2017). Workplace Bullying and Mental Health among Teachers in Relation to Psychosocial Job Characteristics and Burnout. *International Journal of Occupational Medicine and Environmental Health, 30*(4), 629–640. https://doi.org/10.13075/mp.5893.00513

Billett, P., Burns, E., & Foglegarn, R. (2019, May 6). Almost Every Australian Teacher has been Bullied by Students or their Parents, and it's Taking its Toll. *The Conversation.* https://theconversation.com/almost-every-australian-teacher-has-been-bullied-by-students-or-their-parents-and-its-taking-a-toll-116058

Black Dog Institute. (n.d.) *Teachers: The 'Forgotten Frontline' of the pandemic.* https://www.blackdoginstitute.org.au/news/teachers-the-forgotten-frontline-of-the-pandemic/

Boeskens, L., & Nusche, D. (2021). Not enough hours in the day: Policies that shape teachers' use of time. *OECD Education Working Papers, 245.* https://doi.org/10.1787/15990b42-en.

Boulet, M., Wright, B., & Rickinson, M. (2016). *Tackling Avoidable Food Waste in Western Australian Schools: Final Question.* Waste Authority WA. https://www.wasteauthority.wa.gov.au/images/resources/wss/Files/2019/10/WWS_Tackling_Avoidable_Food_Waste_in_WA_Schools_Final_Report.pdf

Brown, M. (2010). *The Presence Process: A Journey Into Present Moment Awareness.* Namaste Publishing.

Buber, M. (1958). *I and Thou.* Scribner.

Buchanan, J. D. (2016). School Micro-Politics and the Beginning Teacher: An Australian Study. *The Social Educator, 34*(2), 21–29.

Burns, E. A., Foglegarn, R., & Billett, P. (2020). Teacher-Targeted Bullying and Harassment in Australian Schools: A Challenge to Teacher Wellbeing. *British Journal of Sociology of Education, 41*(4), 523–538. https://doi.org/10.1080/01425692.2020.1755227

Burrow, R., Williams, R., & Thomas, D. (2020). Stressed, Depressed and Exhausted: Six Years as a Teacher in UK State Education. *Work, Employment and Society, 34*(5), 949–958. https://doi.org/10.1177/0950017020903040

Buyukbayraktar, C. G., & Temiz, G. (2015). The Relationship Between Perfectionism and Burn-Out in Pre-School Teachers. *The Online Journal of New Horizons in Education, 5*(1), 131–148. https://tojned.net/journals/tojned/volumes/tojned-volume05-i01.pdf#page=138

Caleon, I. S., Ilham, N. Q. B., Ong, C. L., & Tan, J. P.-L. (2019). Cascading Effects of Gratitude: A Sequential Mediation Analysis of Gratitude, Interpersonal Relationships, School Resilience and School Well-being. *Asia-Pacific Education Researcher, 28,* 303–312. https://doi.org/10.1007/s40299-019-00440-w

Clegg, S., & Rowland, S. (2010). Kindness in Pedagogical Practice and Academic Life. *British Journal of Sociology of Education, 31*(6), 719–735. https://doi.org/10.1080/01425692.2010.515102

Coles, N. A., Larsen, J. T., & Lench, H. C. (2019). A Meta-Analysis of the Facial Feedback Literature: Effects of Facial Feedback on Emotional Experience are Small and Variable. *Psychological Bulletin, 145*(6), 610–651. https://doi.org/10.1037/bul0000194

Curtiss, P. R., & Warren, P. W. (1973). *The Dynamics of Life Skills Coaching: Life Skills Series.* Training Research and Development Station, Department of Manpower and Immigration.

Dale, M. (2003). Tales In and Out of School. In D. P. Liston & J. W. Garrison (Eds.), *Teaching, Learning and Loving: Reclaiming Passion in Educational Practice* (pp. 65–79). Routledge.

Dempsey, H., Mansfield, C. F., & MacCallum, J. (2020). Early Career Casual Teachers: The Role of Relationships with Colleagues in Negotiating a Teacher Identity and Developing Resilience. In C. F. Mansfield (Ed.), *Cultivating Teacher Resilience* (pp 211–227). Springer.

Digdon, N., & Koble, A. (2011). Effects of Constructive Worry, Imagery Distraction, and Gratitude Interventions on Sleep Quality: A Pilot Trial. *Applied Psychology: Health and Well-Being, 3*(2), 193–206. https://doi.org/10.1111/j.1758-0854.2011.01049.x

Dolev-Cohen, M., & Levkovich, I. (2020). Teachers' Responses to Face-To-Face and Cyberbullying of Colleagues by Others in Israeli Schools. *International Journal of Schools & Educational Psychology, 9*(1), S153–S165. https://doi.org/10.1080/21683603.2020.1772159

Ecclestone, K., & Hayes, D. (2019). *The Dangerous Rise of Therapeutic Education* (2nd ed). Routledge.

Emmons, R. A., & Afshar, M. (2021). Gratitude as the Foundation for Joy. *Journal of Youth and Theology, 20*(1), 5–21. https://doi.org/10.1163/24055093-02001004

Emmons, R. A., & Crumpler, C. A. (2000). Gratitude as a Human Strength: Appraising the Evidence. *Journal of Social and Clinical Psychology, 19*(1), 56–70. https://doi.org/10.1521/jscp.2000.19.1.56

Emmons, R. A., & McCullough, M. E. (Eds.). (2004). *The Psychology of Gratitude*. Oxford University Press.

Emmons, R. A., & Smith, J. A. (2020). What Gratitude is and Why it Matters. In J. A. Smith, K. M. Newman, J. Marsh, & D. Keltner (Eds.), *The Gratitude Project: How the Science of Thankfulness can Rewire our Brains for Resilience, Optimism, and the Greater Good* (pp. 3–11). New Harbinger Publications.

Ewing, L.-A., Ewing, M., & Cooper, H. (2021). From Bad to Worse: The Negative and Deteriorating Portrayal of Teachers on Screen. *Teachers and Teaching, 27*(6), 506–519. https://doi.org/10.1080/13540602.2021.1977270

Falecki, D. & Mann, E. (2020). Practical Applications for Building Teacher Wellbeing in Education. In C. F. Mansfield (Ed.), *Cultivating Teacher Resilience: International Approaches, Applications and Impact* (pp. 175–191). Springer.

Fitzgerald, S., McGrath-Champ, S., Stacey, M., Wilson, R., & Gavin, M. (2018). Intensification of Teachers' Work Under Devolution: A 'Tsunami' of Paperwork. *Journal of Industrial Relations, 61*(5), 613–636. https://doi.org/10.1177/0022185618801396

Fredrickson, B. L. (2004). Gratitude, Like Other Positive Emotions, Broadens and Builds. In R. A. Emmons & M. E. McCullough (Eds.), *The Psychology of Gratitude* (pp. 145–166). Oxford University Press.

Froh, J. J., Bono, G., & Emmons, R. (2010). Beyond Grateful is Beyond Good Manners: Gratitude and Motivation to Contribute to Society Among Early Adolescents. *Motivation and Emotion, 34*, 144–157. https://doi.org/10.1007/s11031-010-9163-z

Grant, A. M., & Gino, F. (2010). A Little Thanks Goes a Long Way: Explaining Why Gratitude Motivate Prosocial Behavior. *Journal of Personality and Social Psychology, 98*(6), 946–955. https://doi.org/10.1037/a0017935

Green Schools Alliance. (n.d.). *About the Green Schools Alliance*. https://www.greenschoolsalliance.org/aboutus

Guan, B., & Jepsen, D. M. (2020). Burnout from Emotional Regulation at Work: The Moderating Role of Gratitude. *Personality and Individual Differences, 156*, 109703. https://doi.org/10.1016/j.paid.2019.109703

Gungor, A., Young, M. E., & Sivo, S. A. (2021). Negative Life Events and Psychological Distress and Life Satisfaction in U.S. College Students: The Moderating Effects of Optimism, Hope, and Gratitude. *Journal of Pedagogical Research, 5*(4), 62–75. https://doi.org/10.33902/JPR.2021472963

Han, B. (2021). The Sources of Organizational Gossips in Schools. *Education Quarterly Reviews, 4*(SI 1), 15–24. https://doi.org/10.31014/aior.1993.04.02.222

Harris, J., Caldwell, B., & Longmuir, F. (2013). *Literature Review: A Culture of Trust Enhances Performance*. Australian Institute for Teaching and School Leadership.

Heffernan, A., Longmuir, F., Bright, D., & Kim, M. (2019). *Perceptions of Teachers and Teaching in Australia*. Monash University. https://www.monash.edu/perceptions-of-teaching/docs/Perceptions-of-Teachers-and-Teaching-in-Australia-report-Nov-2019.pdf

Hemingway, A. P. (2011). How Students' Gratitude for Feedback Can Identify the Right Attitude for Success: Disciplined Optimism. *Perspectives: Teaching Legal Research & Writing, 19*(5), 169–173.

Hemphill, S., Broderick, D., & Heerde, J. (2017). Positive Associations Between School Suspension and Student Problem Behaviour: *Recent Australian Findings. Trends & Issues in Crime and Criminal Justice, 531*. https://www.aic.gov.au/publications/tandi/tandi531

Hlava, P., & Elfers, J. (2013). The Lived Experience of Gratitude. *Journal of Humanistic Psychology, 54*(4). https://doi.org/10.1177/0022167813508605

Howells, K. (2012). *Gratitude in Education: A Radical View*. Sense Publishers.

Howells, K. (2014). An Exploration of the Role of Gratitude in Enhancing Teacher–Student Relationships. *Teaching and Teacher Education, 42*, 58–67. https://doi.org/10.1016/j.tate.2014.04.004

Howells, K. (2018). Developing Gratitude as a Practice for Teachers. In J. R. H. Tudge & L.B. d. L. Freitas (Eds.), *Developing Gratitude in Children and Adolescents* (pp. 240–261). Cambridge University Press.

Howells, K. (2019). The Transformative Power of Gratitude in Education. In B. Shelley, K. te Riele, N. Brown & T. Crellin (Eds.), *Harnessing the Transformative Power of Education* (pp. 180–196). Brill Publishers.

Howells, K. (2021). *Untangling You: How Can I Be Grateful When I Feel so Resentful?*. Major Street Publishing.

Howells, K., & Cumming, J. (2012). Exploring the Role of Gratitude in the Professional Experience of Pre-Service Teachers. *Teaching Education, 23*(1), 71–88.

Howells, K., Stafford, K. E., Guijt, R., & Breadmore, M. (2017). The Role of Gratitude in Enhancing the Relationship Between Doctoral Research Students and their Supervisors. *Teaching in Higher Education, 22*(6), 621– https://doi.org/10.1080/13562517.2016.1273212

Jacobs, L., & de Wet, C. (2018). The Complexity of Teacher-Targeted Workplace Bullying: An Analysis for Policy. *Journal for Juridical Science, 43*(2), 53–78. https://doi.org/10.18820/24150517/JJS43.i2.3

Jackowska, M., Brown, J., Ronaldson, A., & Steptoe, A. (2016). The Impact of a Brief Gratitude Intervention on Subjective Well-Being, Biology and Sleep. *Journal of Health Psychology, 21*(10), 2207–2217. https://doi.org/10.1177/1359105315572455

Jiang, D. (2022). Feeling Gratitude is Associated with Better Well-being Across the Life Span: A Daily Diary Study During the COVID-19 Outbreak. *The Journals of Gerontology: Series B, 77*(4), 36–45. https://doi.org/10.1093/geronb/gbaa220

Johnson, L. (2015). *Teaching Outside the Box* (3rd ed.). Jossey-Bass.

Kaplan, D. M., deBlois, M., Dominguez, V., & Walsh, M. E. (2016). Studying the Teaching of Kindness: A Conceptual Model for Evaluating Kindness Education Programs in Schools. *Evaluation and Program Planning, 58*, 160–170. https://doi.org/10.1016/j.evalprogplan.2016.06.001

Kardaş, F., Çam, Z., Eşkisu, M., & Gelibolu, S. (2019). Gratitude, Hope, Optimism and Life Satisfaction as Predictors of Psychological Well-Being. *Eurasian Journal of Educational Research, 82*, 81–100.

Khatib, H. (2021, August 29). No, Toxic Positivity is not the Same as Gratitude – Here's How to Know the Difference. *Vogue.* https://www.vogue.in/culture-and-living/content/toxic-positivity-versus-gratitude-meaning-difference#:~:text=With%20gratitude%2C%20there%20is%20space,rejecting%20the%20bad%2C%20believes%20Spicer.

Kleinheksel, C. J., & Geisel, R. T. (2019). An Examination of Adult Bullying in the K–12 Workplace: Implications for School Leaders. *School Leadership Review, 14*(1), Article 7.

Klusmann, U., Richter, D., & Lüdtke, O. (2016). Teacher's Emotional Exhaustion is Negatively Related to Students' Achievement: Evidence from a Large-Scale Assessment Study. *Journal of Educational Psychology, 108*(8), 1193–1203. https://doi.org/10.1037/edu0000125

Kõiv, K., & Aia-Utsal, M. (2021, April 24–26). *Victimized Teachers' Experiences About Teacher-Targeted Bullying by Students* [Conference session]. International Psychological Applications Conference and Trends, online. http://inpact-psychologyconference.org/wp-content/uploads/2021/05/2021inpact036.pdf

Komter, A. E. (2004). Gratitude and Gift Exchange. In R. A. Emmons, & M. E. McCullough (Eds.), *The Psychology of Gratitude* (pp. 195–212). Oxford University Press. https://doi.org/10.1093/acprof:oso/9780195150100.003.0010

Korb, A. (2015). *The Upward Spiral: Using Neuroscience to Reverse the Course of Depression, One Small Change at a Time.* New Harbinger Publications.

Lanham, M., Rye, M., Rimsky, L., & Weill, S. (2012). How Gratitude Relates to Burnout and Job Satisfaction in Mental Health Professionals. *Journal of Mental Health Counselling, 34*(4), 341–354. https://doi.org/10.17744/mehc.34.4.w35q80w11kgpqn26

Lara, L., & Saracostti, M. (2019). Effect of Parental Involvement on Children's Academic Achievement in Chile. *Frontiers in Psychology, 10,* Article 1464, 1–5. https://doi.org/10.3389/fpsyg.2019.01464

Lawrence, D. F., Loi, N. M., & Gudex, B. W. (2019). Understanding the Relationship Between Work Intensification and Burnout in Secondary Teachers. Teachers and Teaching: *Theory and Practice, 25*(2), 189–199. https://doi.org/10.1080/13540602.2018.1544551

Lee, J., & Lee, M. (2020). Is 'Whole Child' Education Obsolete? Public School Principals' Educational Goal Priorities in the Era of Accountability. *Educational Administration Quarterly, 56*(5), 856–884. https://doi.org/10.1177/0013161X20909871

Lin, C. (2015). Self-Esteem Mediates the Relationship between Dispositional Gratitude and Well-Being. *Personality and Individual Differences, 85,* 145–148. https://doi.org/10.1016/j.paid.2015.04.045

Lucas, J. (2006). *Retrieving Social Justice as an Aim of Education: The Importance of Dialogical Inquiry* [Doctoral Thesis, University of South Australia]. UniSA Repository. https://find.library.unisa.edu.au/primo-explore/fulldisplay/dedupmrg826614603/ROR

Luu, H. (2020, June 5). *Discover the High School Life in Japan.* SchoolLynk Media. https://schoolynk.com/media/articles/1e6971f4-476e-4632-9b59-0dac44ca068e

Madigan, D. J., & Kim, L. E. (2021). Does Teacher Burnout Affect Students? A Systematic Review of its Association with Academic Achievement and Student-Reported Outcomes. *International Journal of Educational Research, 105,* 101714. https://doi.org/10.1016/j.ijer.2020.101714

Mahmoodi-Shahrebabaki, M. (2016). The Effect of Perfectionism on Burnout among English Language Teachers: The Mediating Role of Anxiety. *Teachers and teaching, 23*(1), 91–105. https://doi.org/10.1080/13540602.2016.1203776

Malone, D. (2017). Socioeconomic Status: A Potential Challenge for Parental Involvement in Schools. *Delta Kappa Gamma Bulletin, 83*(3), 58–62.

McGrath-Champ, S., Wilson, R., Stacey, M., & Fitzgerald, S. (2018). *Understanding Work in Schools: The Foundation for Teaching and Learning 2018 Report to the NSW Teachers Federation*. NSW Teachers Federation. https://hdl.handle.net/2123/21926

McGuire, D. (2021, August 2). Here's Why One-Size-Fits-All Professional Development Is a Waste of Time. *Ed post*. https://www.edpost.com/stories/heres-why-one-size-fits-all-professional-development-is-a-waste-of-time

Naito, T., Matsuda, T., Intasuwan, P., Chuawanlee, W., Thanachanan, S., Ounthitiwat, J., & Fukushima, M. (2010). Gratitude for, and Regret Toward, Nature: Relationships to Proenvironmental Intent of University Students from Japan. *Social Behavior and Personality: An International Journal, 38*(7). 993–1008. https://doi.org/10.2224/sbp.2010.38.7.993

National Center for Mental Health Promotion and Youth Violence Prevention. (2012). *Childhood Trauma and Its Effect on Healthy Development*. https://edn.ne.gov/cms/sites/default/files/u1/pdf/se14Childhood%20Trauma%20%26%20Its%20Effect%20on%20Healthy%20Development.pdf

Nelson, K. (2020). *Wake Up Grateful: The Transformative Practice of Taking Nothing for Granted*. Storey Publishing.

Noddings, N. (1984). *Caring, a Feminine Approach to Ethics and Moral Education*. University of California Press.

Noddings, N. (2005). *The Challenge to Care in Schools: An Alternative Approach to Education* (2nd ed.). Teachers College Press.

Pachler, N., & Broady, E. (2022). Language Policy, Evidence-Informed Practice, the Role of Regulatory Bodies and Teacher Agency. *The Language Learning Journal, 50*(2), 135-141. https://doi.org/10.1080/09571736.2022.2046379

Palmer, P. J. (2017). *The Courage to Teach: Exploring the Inner Landscape of a Teacher's Life, 20th Anniversary Edition*. Jossey-Bass.

Prober, S. M., O'Connor, M. H., & Walsh, F. J. (2011). Australian Aboriginal Peoples' Seasonal Knowledge: A Potential Basis for Shared Understanding in Environmental Management. *Ecology and Society, 16*(2), 1–16. http://www.ecologyandsociety.org/vol16/iss2/art12/

Qiao, B., & Patterson, M. M. (2021). Teachers as Targets of Student Bullying: Data from China and the United States. *Psychology in the Schools, 58*(6), 1133–1150. https://doi.org/10.1002/pits.22493

Rankin, J. G. (2016, November 22). *The Teacher Burnout Epidemic, Part 1 of 2*. Psychology Today. https://www.psychologytoday.com/au/blog/much-more-common-core/201611/the-teacher-burnout-epidemic-part-1-2

Rankin, J. G. (2017, February 1). *The Teacher Burnout Epidemic, Part 2 of 2*. Psychology Today. https://www.psychologytoday.com/au/blog/much-more-common-core/201702/the-teacher-burnout-epidemic-part-2-2

Rankin, L. (n.d.). *Sacred Reciprocity: The Indigenous Spiritual Principle of Giving and Receiving*. https://lissarankin.com/sacred-reciprocity-the-indigenous-spiritual-principle-of-giving-receiving/

Rate My Teachers. (n.d.). *Our Story*. Rate My Teachers. https://ratemyteachers.com/our-story

Redman, T., & Snape, E. (2002). Ageism in Teaching: Stereotypical Beliefs and Discriminatory Attitudes Towards the Over-50s. *Work, Employment and Society, 16*(2), 355–371. https://doi.org/10.1177/095001702400426884

Roberts, R. C. (2004). The Blessings of Gratitude: A Conceptual Analysis. In R. A. Emmons, & M. E. McCullough (Eds.), *The Psychology of Gratitude* (pp. 58–79). Oxford University Press.

Samfira, E. M., & Paloş, R. (2021). Teachers' Personality, Perfectionism, and Self-Efficacy as Predictors for Coping Strategies Based on Personal Resources. *Frontiers in Psychology*. https://doi.org/10.3389/fpsyg.2021.751930

Siegel, D. J. (2014). *Brainstorm: The Power and Purpose of the Teenage Brain*. TarcherPerigee.

Sinha, S., & Yadav, R. (2017). Workplace Bullying in School Teachers: An Indian Enquiry. *Indian Journal of Health and Wellbeing, 8*, 200 –205.

Spender, D. (2007, March 10). Now the Class Scapegoat is the Teacher. *Sydney Morning Herald*. https://www.smh.com.au/national/now-the-class-scapegoat-is-the-teacher-20070310-gdpn47.html

Steindl-Rast, D. (2004). Gratitude as Thankfulness and Gratefulness. In R. A. Emmons, & M. E. McCullough (Eds.), *The Psychology of Gratitude* (pp. 282–290). Oxford University Press.

Taylor, C. (2021). Workplace Bullying: Teacher-on-Teacher. *BU Journal of Graduate Studies in Education, 13*(4), 43–48. https://eric.ed.gov/?id=EJ1306959

TenHouten, W. D. (2018). From Ressentiment to Resentment as a Tertiary Emotion. *Review of European Studies, 10*(4), 49-64. https://doi.org/10.5539/res.v10n4p49

Thomson, S., & Hillman, K. (2019). *The Teaching and Learning International Survey 2018. Australian Report Volume 1: Teachers and School Leaders as Lifelong Learners*. ACER. https://research.acer.edu.au/talis/6/

Tolcher, K., Cauble, M., & Downs, A. (2022). Evaluating the Effects of Gratitude Interventions on College Student Well-being. *Journal of American College Health*, 1–5. https://doi.org/10.1080/07448481.2022.2076096

Tsang, J.-A. (2006). Gratitude and Prosocial Behaviour: An Experimental Test of Gratitude. *Cognition and Emotion, 20*(1), 138–148. https://doi.org/10.1080/02699930500172341

United Nations. (1992). United Nations Framework Convention on Climate Change. https://unfccc.int/files/essential_background/background_publications_htmlpdf/application/pdf/conveng.pdf

University of Bath. (2022, January 5). *Government Inaction on Climate Change Linked to Psychological Distress in Young People – New Study*. https://www.bath.ac.uk/announcements/government-inaction-on-climate-change-linked-to-psychological-distress-in-young-people-new-study/

Ure, M. (2014). Resentment/Ressentiment. *Constellations*, 22(4) 599–613. https://doi.org/10.1111/1467-8675.12098

Vaughan, G., & Estola, E. (2007). The Gift Paradigm in Early Childhood Education. *Educational Philosophy and Theory, 39*(3), 246–263. https://doi.org/10.1111/j.1469-5812.2007.00326.x

Vernon, L. L., Dillon, J. M., & Steiner, A. R. W. (2009). Proactive Coping, Gratitude, and Posttraumatic Stress Disorder in College Women. *Anxiety, Stress, & Coping, 22*(1), 117–127. https://doi.org/10.1080/10615800802203751

Vieselmeyer, J., Holguin J., & Mezulis, A. (2017). The Role of Resilience and Gratitude in Posttraumatic Stress and Growth Following a Campus Shooting. *Psychological Trauma: Theory, Research Practice, and Policy, 9*(1), 62–69. https://doi.org/10.1037/tra0000149

Visser, M. (2009). *The Gift of Thanks: The Roots and Rituals of Gratitude*. Houghton Mifflin Harcourt.

Watkins, P. C. (2014). *Gratitude and the Good Life: Toward a Psychology of Appreciation*. Springer.

Watkins, P. C., & McCurrach, D. (2016). Exploring how Gratitude Trains Cognitive Processes Important to Well-being. In D. Carr (Ed.), *Perspectives on Gratitude: An Interdisciplinary Approach* (pp. 27–40). Routledge.

Wong, J. Y., Owen, J., Gabana, N. T., Brown, J. W., McInnis, S., Toth, P, & Gilman, L. (2016). Does Gratitude Writing Improve the Mental Health of Psychotherapy Clients? Evidence from a Randomized Controlled Trial. *Psychotherapy Research, 28*, 1–11. https://doi.org/10.1080/10503307.2016.1169332

Wood, A. M., Joseph, S., & Linley, P. A. (2007). Coping Style as a Psychological Resource of Grateful People. *Journal of Social and Clinical Psychology, 26*(9), 1076–1093. https://doi.org/10.1521/jscp.2007.26.9.1076

Wood, A. M., Froh, J. J., & Geraghty, A. W. A. (2010). Gratitude and Well-Being: A Review and Theoretical Integration. *Clinical Psychology Review, 30*(7), 890–905. https://doi.org/10.1016/j.cpr.2010.03.005

Woodward, E., & McTaggart P. M. (2019). Co-developing Indigenous Seasonal Calendars to Support 'Healthy Country, Healthy People' Outcomes. *Global Health Promotion, 26*(3 supp). https://doi.org/10.1177/1757975919832241

World Health Organization. (2021). *Global Report on Ageism*. World Health Organization.

World Wildlife Fund (WWF). (2019). *Food Waste Warriors: A Deep Dive into Food Waste in US Schools*. World Wildlife Fund.

Index

A

acceptance
    and gratitude, 7, 44, 48, 82
    and humility, 42
    and limitations, 46, 62, 134
    and resentment, 83
    spirit of, 41–43
    and staff behaviour, 67, 74, 101
    the status quo, 55, 81
achievements and successes
    acknowledge and celebrate, 36, 42, 90, 138
    impacts on, 24
    measurements of, 125
    notice and reflect on, 34, 42, 46, 57, 61, 132
    students', 24, 78, 90, 126
ageism, 95–97, 101, 102
anxiety and stress
    beginning teachers, 39
    environmental issues, 110–111, 113, 115, 120
    and gratitude, 16, 31, 115, 121, 137
    and mental health, 38
    and personal disposition, 27
    and positivity, 26
attitude, inner
    and change, 55–56, 72–73, 82, 83
    and choice, 128
    and gratitude, 15–16, 55–57, 58, 60, 61, 103, 119, 128, 138–139
    identity and integrity, 56
    impacts of, 57, 60, 101–103
    and natural environment, 112, 121
    and perspectives, 74
    and preparedness, 57
    and self-gratitude, 57–58
    and workload, 20–21

B

Barker & Harris (2020), 78, 79, 89
beginning teachers
    and anxiety, 39
    collegial relationships, 43
    discouragement, 100
    expectations, 42, 48, 134
    mentors, 39
    motivation, 66, 111, 129–130
belonging, sense of, 72, 88
binary thinking, 70, 116–117, 120, 121
bullying and harassment
    impacts of, 52–53, 65
    online, 52
    school administration reaction, 65
    students' roles in, 52
    workplace, 64–65

C

challenges
    difficult relationships, 68
    education systems, 59, 126–127, 131, 137
    as gifts, 31
    limitations, 62
    and motivation, 47

parent and teacher communications, 79–80
for parents, 88
school culture, 64, 66
sociocultural, 88
change
    attitudinal, 81–82
    environmental preservation, 117
    and gratitude, 7–8, 104, 138
    inner attitude, 56–57, 82
    and resentment, 91
    role of humility, 73
    self-efficacy, 56
climate change and environmental issues
    Australian Curriculum, 110, 114
    First Nations knowledge, 112, 119–120
    The Green Schools Alliance, 111
    impact of like-minded people, 115–116
    and mental health, 110–111
    resentment, 112
collegial relationships
    accepting support, 30, 71
    ageism, 95–96, 102
    and binary thinking, 70, 116
    and blame, 73
    damaging actions, 100
    developing and improving, 32, 60, 66, 101, 104, 134
    difficult, 51, 63–64, 69
    and feedback, 45
    and gratitude, 68, 69
    impacts, 40–41, 43, 67, 70, 74
    inclusivity, 104
    motivation, 101
    and perfectionist teachers, 38
    perspectives, 66, 70, 71, 74, 134
    receiving and giving, 30
    reconnaissance, 71, 75
    reflect on, 69, 75, 101–103
    resentment, 63, 64, 97–98
    and resilience, 67–68
    and staff morale, 70
    stressful, 39
    supportive, 42, 57, 59
    and timetabling, 64
competence
    consciously competent, 43
    consciously incompetent stage, 48
    unconscious incompetence, 42
confidence, impacts on, 24, 26, 40, 51–52, 78, 98, 101
COVID lockdowns, 79, 96
cultural barriers, 79

D

deep gratitude
    challenges, 58
    and change, 7
    cycle of, 27, 34
    defined, 3–4, 15
    and giving, 36
    impacts on, 58, 137
    and inner attitude, 32–33, 55–56
    non-reciprocal dimension, 4
    and perfectionist mode, 38
    and personal wellbeing, 28
    and perspectives, 5, 16
    and positivity, 3, 26, 28
    power of, 6, 9, 31, 138–139
    proactive gratitude, 35
    small steps, 36
    and the state of being, 56
    see also gratitude
discovery mode, 47–48, 49

E

education systems
- change, 109, 134
- consumer mentality, 64
- cultures, 125
- depersonalising, 133
- expectations, 133, 134–135
- and gratitude, 128, 130, 132, 137–138
- limitations, 59, 126–127, 131

empathy
- and binary thinking, 117
- developing, 74–75
- and difficult relationships, 71
- gratitude practice, 46, 131, 138
- and perspectives, 74
- and reconnaissance, 71

environment, natural
- connections with, 118, 120
- gratitude, 113, 119–121
- impacts of, 113
- and inner attitude, 112, 121

environmental issues and climate change
- Australian Curriculum, 110, 114
- First Nations knowledge, 112, 119–120
- and mental health, 110–111
- United Nations Conference on Environment and Development (1992), 110

environmental preservation
- activists, 120
- The Green Schools Alliance, 111
- impact of like-minded people, 115–116
- and resentment, 112

environments, school
- and change, 33
- culture, 33, 64, 66, 102

education programs, 109
- and negativity, 63, 65, 74
- positive, 57, 104
- waste management, 110–112, 114, 121

expectations
- beginning teachers, 42, 48, 134
- and disappointments, 70, 84, 92, 127, 131
- giving and receiving, 4
- and gratitude, 9, 28–29, 33, 91, 137
- impacts of, 77
- and parents, 78, 86–89
- reflect on, 85
- in relationships, 40, 99–100
- of teachers, 13, 21, 54, 82–83, 85, 96–97, 126
- unrealistic, 6, 38, 43, 96–97

F

failure, sense of
- and collegial relationships, 37, 39, 70
- and gratitude, 9, 32
- impacts of, 5, 25–26
- and perfectionist mode, 44
- and self-care, 34
- students, 79
- in teaching, 57–59, 128

feedback
- accepting, 43–45
- from colleagues, 39, 101
- explicit, 90
- and perfectionist mode, 47
- positive reinforcement, 45
- reflection, 48
- seek, 48–49, 75

G

giving and receiving, 3, 4, 29, 30, 36, 44

gratitude
- and acceptance, 7, 41–42, 44, 48, 55
- accessing, 26, 29
- and anxiety, 31, 115, 121, 137
- and change, 91, 104
- circle of, 29, 31
- and collegial relationships, 1, 68, 69, 117, 136
- dimensions, 3
- and empathy, 46, 117, 131, 138
- environmental impacts, 55
- and expectations, 9, 28–29, 33, 91, 137
- and humility, 42, 73, 128
- impacts, 7, 15–16, 27, 28, 32, 41, 61, 82, 116, 117, 137–138
- and inner attitude, 15–16, 32–33, 55–57, 58, 60, 61, 103, 119, 128, 138–139
- and kindness, 29, 32, 35, 96, 104–105
- misconceptions, 27, 55
- and motivation, 3, 9, 110, 112, 121, 129, 137
- and natural environment, 113, 119–121
- and negativity, 26, 31, 41, 70–71
- and parents, 88–89, 90–91, 137
- and perfectionist mode, 39–40
- and perspectives, 38, 47, 138
- and positive thinking, 26, 28–29, 35
- reciprocation, 4, 91
- and resentment, 5, 67, 73, 82, 99, 106, 138
- and resilience, 4–5, 113, 128
- scepticism of, 8
- and self-acceptance, 46
- small steps, 32, 33–34, 67, 71, 133
- sociocultural influences, 2
- and stress, 27, 31, 115, 121, 137
- systemic constraints, 7–8, 128
- *see also* deep gratitude

gratitude practices
- appreciation and thankfulness, 32
- attentive listening, 117, 120, 121
- critiquing, 103
- empathy, 70–71, 131, 138
- and the environment, 113, 118, 120, 121
- and imperfections, 45
- interpersonal, 34
- journaling, 8, 31, 33–35, 121, 136
- noticing, 29–30, 35, 46, 48, 96, 107, 136
- openness, 35
- positive reinforcement, 45
- positive salutations, 73
- reconnaissance, 71–74, 75, 101, 105–106
- recording gratitude, 36, 72
- and self-efficacy, 123
- self-gratitude, 33, 34, 46, 128, 131
- speaking your truth, 130–131, 136

H

habits
- and gratitude, 16, 20–22
- procrastination, 16–17
- regular and sustained, 4

harassment
- impacts of, 52–53, 65
- online, 52
- school administration support, 65
- students' roles in, 52
- workplace, 64–65

health and wellbeing
- and angry students, 51
- and gratitude, 27, 28
- gratitude journal, 31, 33–35
- impacts on, 12, 24, 68
- and negativity, 51–52
- and perfectionist mode, 38
- self-care, 28, 33
- sleep, 33–34
- and stress, 38
- work-life balance, 25
- workload, 124

humility
- in collegial relationships, 69
- competence stages, 42–43, 48
- and gratitude, 73, 128, 142
- personal disposition, 105
- as receiver, 29

I

inferiority, sense of
- and collegial relationships, 42, 95–96, 98–100, 102
- and gratitude, 106
- from words, 104, 107

inner attitude
- change, 55–56, 72–73, 82, 83, 128
- environmental gratitude, 112, 121
- and gratitude, 15–16, 32–33, 55–57, 58, 60, 61, 103, 119, 128, 138–139
- identity and integrity, 56
- impacts of, 57, 60, 101–103
- negativity, 73
- perspectives, 74
- and preparedness, 57
- self-gratitude, 57–58

J

job satisfaction, 11, 24, 63, 65
journaling, 8, 91, 121, 136, 138

K

kindness
- and discovery mode, 47
- and gratitude, 29, 32, 35, 96, 104–105
- in relationships, 107
- to yourself, 9, 47, 61–62

L

language
- in communication, 87
- in educational discourse, 99, 101
- and gratitude, 41
- habits, 17
- impacts of, 20, 57, 60, 99, 100, 102–104, 107
- and kindness, 104
- school culture, 102

M

media representations of teaching, 95, 96
motivation
- and ageism, 101
- beginning teachers, 66, 111, 129–130
- from challenges, 138

and gratitude, 3, 9, 110, 112, 121, 137
impacts, 16, 24, 32, 119
and imperfections, 47
maintaining, 114, 135
and natural environment, 113
and professional identity, 68
multitasking, 17–18, 21, 22

N

nature *see* environment, natural
negativity
    in behaviours, 71
    and collegial relationships, 66
    and gratitude, 26, 31, 41, 70–71
    impacts of, 12, 40, 48, 51–52, 103
    impacts on students, 15, 24
    inner attitude, 73
    in the media, 95, 96
    from perfectionism, 38, 43
    and positive thinking, 26–29, 35
    and school environments, 63, 65
    and self-talk, 48
Noddings (1984), 87
Noddings (2005), 29

O

Organisation for Economic Co-operation and Development (OECD), 12

P

parents and carers
    barriers, 87
    communications, 78, 84–88, 90, 92
    COVID lockdowns, 79
    expectations, 84–88
    feedback, 45
    and gratitude, 90–91, 93, 137
    impacts, 64, 77–79, 80–81
    judgements of, 82–83
    nurturing engagement, 89
    and the perfectionist teacher, 44
    perspectives, 87, 91
    reconnaissance, 86, 91–92
    resentment towards, 80, 90, 92
perfectionist mode
    accepting feedback, 44
    and competency stages, 43
    flawed, 37, 45
    and gratitude, 39–40
    impacts of, 38, 40
    and imperfections, 49
    perspective, 49
    self-awareness, 46
    and self-gratitude, 46
    and *wabi-sabi* (Japanese), 45, 49
perspectives
    changes, 16, 47–49, 60, 68, 70, 110, 128
    choices, 81–82
    and collegial relationships, 66, 70, 71, 74, 134
    and empathy, 74
    impacts of, 131, 138
    learning from, 5, 91, 107, 117
    the nature of time, 21
    in parent relationships, 84, 87
    of past and future, 120
    workload management, 22
positivity, 3, 26, 27, 35, 45
preparedness, state of, 6, 56–57, 119
presence and state of being, 19–20, 22, 31, 56

R

receiving and giving, 3, 4, 29, 30, 36, 44
reconnaissance, 71–74, 75, 85–86, 101, 105–106
research, studies and surveys
    ageism, 97–98
    bullying, 52, 54, 65, 79
    giving and receiving mode, 29–30
    grateful disposition, 27, 44
    gratitude and sleep quality, 34
    impacts of gratitude, 1, 2, 15, 31, 68, 104, 106
    impacts of trauma, 54
    impacts of work-related stress, 24
    impacts on students, 24, 113
    media representations of teaching, 96
    and perfectionist mode, 38, 40
    and personal disposition, 27
    professional development, 124–125
    reactions to climate change, 110
    recording gratitude, 31
    smiling, 34
    student achievements, 12
    teacher mental health, 96–97
    teacher stress, 24
    teacher workloads, 12, 14, 96–97
    waste in schools, 111
resentment
    and belittling behaviours, 106
    and blame, 73, 135
    and change, 91
    and collegial relationships, 63, 64, 97–98
    and disempowerment, 127–128
    and environmental issues, 112
    and gratitude, 5, 67, 73, 82, 99, 138
    and humility, 69
    impacts, 67, 81, 102–103
    and inner attitude, 83
    ownership of, 103
    and perspectives, 128
    and power struggles, 99
    and shock, 83–84
    towards parents, 80
resilience
    building, 2, 23, 34, 60, 110, 115, 120, 132
    and collegial relationships, 67–68
    and gratitude, 4–5, 113, 128
    and journaling, 136
    in schools, 68
    in students, 87

S

school environments
    and change, 33
    culture, 33, 64, 66, 102
    education programs, 109
    and negativity, 63, 65, 74
    positive, 57, 104
    waste management, 110–112, 114, 121
self-efficacy, 24, 52, 56, 73, 109
Spender (2007), 124
stress
    beginning teachers, 39
    environmental issues, 110–111, 113, 115, 120
    and gratitude, 16, 27, 31, 115, 121, 137
    impacts on student achievements, 24

and mental health, 38
and motivation, 24
and personal disposition, 27
and positivity, 26
students
    angry, 51–52, 60
    bullying and harassment, 52
    connectedness, 57, 82, 104
    feedback, 45
    and gratitude, 137
    impacts of language, 102
    and perfectionist teachers, 38
    resilience, 87
    social impacts on, 52
studies, surveys and research
    ageism, 97–98
    bullying, 52, 54, 65, 79
    giving and receiving mode, 29–30
    grateful disposition, 27, 44
    gratitude and sleep quality, 34
    impacts of gratitude, 1, 2, 15, 31, 68, 104, 106
    impacts of trauma, 54
    impacts of work-related stress, 24
    impacts on students, 24, 113
    media representations of teaching, 96
    and perfectionist mode, 38, 40
    and personal disposition, 27
    professional development, 124–125
    reactions to climate change, 110
    recording gratitude, 31
    smiling, 34
    student achievements, 12
    teacher mental health, 96–97
    teacher stress, 24
    teacher workloads, 12, 14, 96–97
    waste in schools, 111
successes and achievements
    acknowledge and celebrate, 36, 42, 90, 138
    impacts on, 24
    measurements of, 125
    notice and reflect on, 34, 42, 57, 61, 132
    students', 24, 78, 90, 126

T

teachers
    accepting feedback, 43–44
    building resilience, 2, 34
    and confidence, 43–44
    developing gratitude skills, 9
    exhaustion and stress, 24
    expectations of, 13, 21, 54, 126
    job satisfaction, 11, 24, 63, 65
    and motivation, 129–130
    multitasking, 17
    non-teaching workload, 12–13
    objectified, 99–100
    professional development, 124–125, 129
    relationships with students, 61
    and resentment, 135
    self-care, 33
    self-efficacy, 24, 109
    self-gratitude, 131
    sense of inadequacy, 32, 34, 37, 39, 44, 57–59, 70, 99, 128
    as service providers, 99
    workloads, 11–12, 25, 124–126, 129
    see also collegial relationships

teaching
- bullying and harassment, 52
- consciously competent, 43
- and COVID lockdowns, 79
- impacts of perfectionist mode and anxiety, 38, 42, 44, 47
- impacts of reflection, 45, 103
- impacts of technology, 7–8, 95, 97–98, 103, 124
- impacts of workload, 33–34
- and mentors, 39
- motivation, 24, 68, 129–130, 136
- positive moments, 1–2
- professional standards, 64
- society views, 52, 95–96, 124
- stressors, 24
- and student achievement, 24
- support, 109, 126–127
- systemic constraints, 7–8, 14, 123
- unconscious incompetence, 42

Teaching and Learning International Survey (TALIS), 12

technology, impacts on teaching, 7–8, 78, 95, 97–98, 103, 124

time
- and gratitude, 17–18
- impact of language habits, 17
- impacts of distractions, 16
- prioritising, 18–19, 22
- and procrastination, 16–17
- relationship with, 16, 19, 20–22
- and sense of being present, 20
- time-poor, 11–13

U

United Nations Conference on Environment and Development (1992), 110

W

Watkins (2014), 27, 41

Watkins and McCurrach (2016), 40, 41

wellbeing and health
- and angry students, 51
- and gratitude, 27, 28
- gratitude journal, 31, 33–35
- impacts on, 12, 24, 68
- and negativity, 51–52
- and perfectionist mode, 38
- self-care, 28, 33
- sleep, 33–34
- and stress, 38
- workload, 124

Woodward & McTaggart (2019), 119–120

words
- in communication, 87
- in educational discourse, 99, 101
- and gratitude, 41
- habits, 17
- impacts of, 20, 57, 60, 99, 100, 102–104, 107
- and kindness, 104
- school culture, 102

work-life balance, 19, 21, 33–34

worthiness, sense of, 72, 96, 125

Acknowledgements

With a heart of gratitude, we would like to acknowledge the teachers and educators that we work with daily. Their inspiring and courageous stories have enriched this book and our writing journey.

We thank Jacinta Dietrich from Hawker Brownlow for her editorial assistance. We also acknowledge Lynden Howells for his time and careful attention in proofreading and editing final manuscripts of this book.

Finally, we would like to express our sincere gratitude to our friends and family, and in particular our husbands, Lynden Howells and Patrick Curley, for their unwavering support and encouragement.

About the authors

Dr Kerry Howells is an award-winning educator and author with over 25 years of experience in researching, teaching and practising gratitude. Working with school leaders and teachers in many countries, Kerry has embedded gratitude in diverse contexts and at all levels of education. Her work is underpinned by a deep philosophical exploration of gratitude, particularly focusing on finding practical applications in the face of difficulties. Kerry has published widely in academic papers in the areas of school leadership and teaching, pre-service teacher education, indigenous education, early childhood education and academic learning. Her recent book *Untangling you: How can I be grateful when I feel so resentful?* has won four international awards and is now available in many languages.

Dr Jo Lucas is currently a teacher in Big Picture at Hobart City High School, Tasmania. Jo has worked as a classroom teacher for seventeen years in primary and secondary settings. Jo combined this role with her work as an educational researcher and pre-service teacher educator in universities, and mentor for beginning teachers in schools. Jo has undertaken research, writing and consultancy in areas such as: retrieving social justice as an aim of education; teachers' perspectives on the nature of a quality teaching environment; Australian Aboriginal studies and anti-racist education; ethical inquiry and philosophy for children; and alternative university entrance programs for senior secondary students. Jo has also worked for the Australian Education Union advocating for improved industrial conditions for new educators.

www.ingramcontent.com/pod-product-compliance
Lightning Source LLC
Chambersburg PA
CBHW050233120526
44590CB00016B/2075